Gunner Kaye

An artilleryman's experiences
from the Normandy Beaches to VE Day

For Myra

and

Harri and Hannah

They shall not grow old
As we that are left grow old
Age shall not weary them
Nor the years condemn
At the going down of the sun
And in the morning
We will remember them

Gunner Kaye

First Edition – December 2007

Published by Geoff Blore Publishing

Geoff Blore Publishing
19 Hillside
Ludlow
Shropshire
SY8 1RB

Email: doolbykid@aol.com

Book set in Times New Roman 12pt

Graphic Design and Print Management by
Print by Design Ltd, Bodmin, Cornwall UK
www.printbydesign.co.uk

ISBN 978-0-9557830-0-5

To buy direct go to www.gunnerkaye.com

Contents

All photographs unless otherwise stated are courtesy of Ron Kaye. All maps by Willy Kaye.

Introduction
and
Acknowledgments

In September 2002 I was relaxing in a bar in Arromanches, Normandy, after a thoroughly enjoyable day visiting the sites immortalised by the Allied landings on 6th June 1944, D-Day. By 10pm only a few locals and myself remained, so I decided to finish my drink, head back to the hotel, and get myself ready for the next day's itinerary. No sooner had I made that decision, than three men entered the bar.

Two were around my age, but the third was an older man. Overhearing them order their drinks, I realised they were English, and in time, I approached their table and asked if they would mind me joining them. They graciously agreed, and introduced themselves. This was the day that I first met Ronald 'Danny' Kaye, the reason that you are now reading these words.

I soon learned that Danny (he has been universally known by his nickname since the 1950's) was a D-Day veteran, and that he and his son and grandson, Willy and Jolyon respectively, were in France for a ceremony to honour the regiment he had served with during the Second World War. It was a real treat for me to talk to an actual veteran, and over the next few hours we chatted about his memories from that time. At some point in the conversation, I mentioned that I had written the memoirs of an

1

old soldier from my locality, prompting Willy to casually suggest that I write Danny's. I agreed that it was a very interesting proposal, and we decided to pursue the idea when we returned to Britain.

Once home, I thought long and hard about taking the project on. It would be a difficult assignment, made harder by the fact that I lived so far from Danny, but in the end I couldn't resist it. I felt that it was a story that had to be told. Within a few weeks I had travelled to Danny's home in Shropshire, where I received a warm welcome from him and his wife Joan. For the next two days, with the tape rolling, I recorded the main elements of the story.

On returning to Wales, with the help of the taping sessions, I began developing the basic framework of the book and over the following months I spent many hours on the phone with Danny quizzing him about his experiences. The task then was to build his story into the wider picture, so the reader would have the opportunity to see the battle from both perspectives. I hope I have achieved this.

The scale of the project proved daunting at times, but I received great encouragement from Danny and his family, especially his son Willy, who has been a constant source of inspiration, and provided a great deal of practical help, as many of the maps included in the book are his creation. I am indebted to him.

Another tremendous source of help was Colonel John Sainsbury, whose detailed reference work on the Hertfordshire Yeomanry Regiments of the Royal Artillery, proved critical to the development of this book. His candour and insightful suggestions got me back on track at a difficult time, and gave me fresh enthusiasm for the project. I could not have completed it without his help.

I would also like to thank Geoff Blore, the publisher, for his interest and enthusiasm for the project, and John Slipper for his design contributions.

Love and thanks go to my wife Adele, who has encouraged me, and given me the time I needed to complete the project.

Lastly, I want to thank Danny. I hope that all who read this book feel the same pride and gratitude I felt during its development. It is an honour to tell his story.

To quote Bill Clinton, who once said of the Normandy veterans, 'let us not forget that, when these men were young, they saved the world.'

Simon Evans

August 2003

4

Chapter One

Starting out

13th March 1923 – 28th January 1942

Ronald James Kaye came into the world in the early hours of March 13th 1923, the second child born to Mary Teresa Kaye and Percy James Kaye, a carter at the nearby railway yard at Wallasey, on the Wirral, opposite the hustle and bustle of the Liverpool docks and shipyards.

The family home, a three-bedroom terraced house in Charlotte Road, (the 'posh-end' as Ron calls it), was much the same as the others in the area. Nobody had a great deal of money, but it was a tight community of hard working people, struggling to recover from the after effects of the Great War.

"Times were hard yes, but we always had enough. Everyone was in the same boat so you don't really notice then."

Ron's early school years were spent at Church Street Primary in nearby Manor Road. School was something he endured rather than enjoyed; classes never held the same excitement for him as sports, something that was well catered for at that time, not only in Birkenhead, but also in the surrounding area of Liverpool.

"There was always plenty going on and plenty to do. My dad used to take us to the stadium in Liverpool on a Thursday night to watch the wrestling, or we'd go on a Friday for the boxing. There was wrestling at the Tower in New Brighton, as well, and sometimes he'd take us over there.

We'd go to the big football matches too, Liverpool and Everton games. I can remember seeing Dixie Dean, the Everton centre-forward play; and Fred Lawton who played in goal. We used to go and watch our local side, New Brighton, too.

There were a lot of attractions around the area where we lived, funfairs and rides, a boating lake, Central Park, things like that. There was a lot going on. I'd go with my pals or my brothers and sister and we'd go over to New Brighton and swim across the Mersey to the boats. After a bit of a rest, we'd swim back again. I was a good swimmer; I always loved the water."

Despite the distractions, Ronnie, like most young lads, had his fair share of scrapes with the law.

"You know, we had a very happy childhood. My dad was a very strict man but he was very fair too, and thank God he was, because the police were very often knocking at our door!

It was never for anything serious though, just pranks really. Back then, if the 'bobbies' caught you up to no good they'd ask you 'what do you want? A 'clacking' off me or shall I go to see your dad?' 'Go and see my dad' I'd say! It didn't really matter though because half the time they'd say 'Bugger that, you'll get one anyway!' They'd clip your ear and tell you to get off."

When the time came for him to leave school Ron took on a variety of jobs. In due course he worked as a 'grocers lad', a paperboy and in the local butcher's shop.

"I did all right there. I worked my way up to first lad

7

behind the counter but then I got the chance to go and
work in the building trade and I jumped at it because
I'd always wanted an outdoor job."

It was 1939 and Ron was sixteen years old. Things were going well, he had a good job and he was happy, but events were about to unfold which would dramatically alter his future. In September of that year, barely twenty years after the end of the horrors of the Great War, Europe was once again plunged into darkness by the consequences of the German invasion of Poland. Adolf Hitler, the leader of the ruling Nazi Party, had in the six years since he had become Chancellor secretly re-armed the nation and had almost miraculously revived the ruined economy. Germany was once again a prosperous, confident country, albeit totally dominated by its fuhrer.

Trouble had been brewing for some time now. After being elected Chancellor, Hitler had withdrawn Germany from the League of Nations, a kind of forerunner to the United Nations. No sooner had he done this, he began to lay claim to vast areas of land that had been taken from Germany at the end of the First World War, as part of the massive war reparations that had been imposed on the country.

Britain, itself still recovering from the previous conflict, had neither the desire nor the resources for another war, and adopted a policy of appeasement. As Hitler occupied the Rhineland and later annexed Austria, Britain and France stood idle, hoping he would be satisfied with these gains. It was only later when parts of Czechoslovakia were occupied that they finally realised the gravity of the situation, and as Hitler began to turn his attention to Poland, Britain reluctantly declared that it would guarantee Polish sovereignty if the need arose.

On September 1st 1939 that need arose. The German forces, having now mobilised approximately six million men, swarmed over the Polish border, using terrifying new tactics called 'Blitzkrieg', or 'lightning war'. This revolutionary use of tanks, planes and infantry in a combined role completely overwhelmed the Poles and within days the country had capitulated.

Britain and France had declared war on Germany as soon as she had invaded Poland but for the minute offered their ally no material assistance. Instead, Britain began shipping 158,000 men and 25,000 vehicles across the Channel to help defend France, which would be relying heavily on its much-vaunted Maginot Line, a series of heavily armed fortifications along the border with Germany, to repel any invasion. The next six months became known as 'the phoney war', or 'sitzkrieg'. Nothing happened in the West.

In the East however plans were being made, and on 10th May 1940 the Germans struck west into Holland and Belgium and, into France through the Ardennes, a heavily wooded region deemed totally unsuitable for tanks by the Allied leaders. Superior tactics and dynamic leadership on the German side soon resulted in the Allied forces being forced back to the area of Dunkirk on the French coast. By June 4th, amid terrible fighting, 338,226 soldiers from Britain, France and Belgium had been evacuated to the UK, in every size and type of vessel that could be mustered for the operation. On the beaches behind them however, they'd had to abandon vast numbers of tanks, vehicles, and guns and equipment that would lead to critical shortages for some time after.

Having seen off the British, the Germans turned their attention to the French who realising that they could not halt the onslaught, surrendered two weeks later on 21st June. With the fall of France, Hitler was master of Western Europe; but it wasn't enough. As he gazed across the English Channel from the shores of his latest conquest, he was already thinking of his next move. Britain would not surrender - that had been made very clear. He would have to invade the island, but to do so successfully he would need control of the skies. The aerial onslaught would soon begin.

The summer of 1940 was a fight to the finish between the R.A.F. and the Luftwaffe, in which the latter came off worse. Despite their best efforts, the German pilots could not gain the necessary mastery of the air and the invasion was postponed indefinitely. Both sides now adopted a different strategy—the crippling of each other's ability to make war. The 'Blitz' on Britain's cities was about to begin.

Considering its location and importance to the British war effort, Liverpool was an obvious target for the German bombers. Night after night the skies over the city were filled with the ominous drone of the Junkers, Heinkels and Dorniers, while anti-aircraft batteries fought desperately to shoot them down before they could unload their deadly cargo onto the city and the docks.

"We'd had some bombing in 1940 but it was in March of '41 that they really hammered us. It went on for weeks and that was when our house got hit. It was amazing really that none of us was hurt because the blast from the bomb knocked our chimneystack right down into the living room.

There was a hell of a mess and the house was considered unsafe, so we moved shortly afterwards to Lee Road, which was a similar place. I think they rebuilt the house in Charlotte Road after the war."

The almost surreal days of the 'phoney war' seemed a lifetime away and the British public was now locked in a grim struggle for survival. Rationing of food and petrol had been introduced, and the pre-war measure of conscription, initially applying to men between the ages of 20–27, was soon raised to 36 years of age as the crisis deepened.

Ron was under age, and thus not eligible for call-up, but he decided to enlist anyway.

"I went along with my mates to an Army recruiting office in Birkenhead and joined up. I had to lie about my age, but I didn't want to stay in Wallasey because most of my mates had gone by then. One had gone in the Navy and he was only sixteen! My brother Fred had joined earlier as well so I wanted to go too. Anyway I gave them a false age and had the medical, and I passed! I was in.

To be truthful the Army wasn't my first choice. What I really wanted to do was join the RAF but I was told that basically I had no chance because I hadn't had a proper education - grammar school and that - so I just forgot all about it and settled for the Army."

Now came the difficult part, as Ron hadn't considered one important detail of his plan; he hadn't told his parents about what he intended to do.

"Well after a few days the acceptance letter turned up in the post without me knowing and when my mam saw the OHMS stamp on the envelope she opened it and found out what I'd done.

The thing was, she didn't say anything to me about it. She hid the letter 'til my dad got home from work! After he'd seen it he took me straight back down to the recruiting office and exposed my real age. That was it - I couldn't go. See, my dad had served in the First World War, at Ypres and Salonika, and he didn't want the same for me. Looking back it was a bit of a blessing because if I'd gone in then I'd have been in the Cheshires, an infantry regiment."

Disappointed but not yet ready to give up, Ron discovered another way to contribute to the war effort.

"Well I thought that if I can't go in the Army I'd find another way to do my bit. I went down to the L.D.V. recruiting office in Wallasey with my Uncle Jack, who was well into his forties and already a member, and

signed on. Not long after, a couple of days, I got a letter telling me I was in and where and when I should report."

The Local Defence Volunteers was created on 14th May 1940 after the government had broadcast a message asking for volunteers for a nationwide part-time, unpaid force. Within a month 750,000 men had volunteered, and by July this figure had risen to over one million. The government was sure that the L.D.V. could play an important role in safeguarding the nation's security, by helping to delay any invasion force for as long as possible. The time bought would in theory, give the regular army's mobile formations the chance to engage the enemy on grounds of their choosing. The extent to which the Home Guard, as the LDV was renamed on Churchill's insistence in August 1940, could really contribute to holding up the invaders was limited to their inadequate arms, but as time went on it became a well-equipped and useful organisation.

"Being a young lad I was always paired up with an older bloke. I was working as a builder at the time so after work, two or three times a week, you'd be on duty, and in twos or threes you'd go out on patrol or guard duty. We had to keep an eye on everything in the area, but especially the beaches, docks, bridges and the important roads.

I don't know what we'd have done if it had come to it 'cos we didn't have any guns! There was only one weapon for the entire unit, an old Ross rifle if I remember. I think it might have been a First World War gun or even before that! We never even shot with it! It was just to practice with. We learned to strip it and clean it and things like that.

Not long before I left they had some new equipment in and a few more rifles. We were issued a uniform though, and when I left they let me keep it. "

Ron's stint in the Home Guard was about to come to an abrupt end. Around Christmas of 1941, not long after the United States had entered the war; following the Japanese attack on its naval fleet at Pearl Harbour in the Pacific, another letter bearing the OHMS stamp arrived at the Kaye household in Lee Road.

"It was just before or just after Christmas that I got the 'call-up letter'. This time there was nothing that my dad could do about it cos I was old enough now. It meant another trip back to Birkenhead for a medical. It was the day after New Years Day, January 2nd, and that's where I first met John Mason.

We just hit it off from the start and formed a firm friendship. We both passed the medical 'A1' and before we left we swapped addresses. Over the next few weeks he'd come over to my place for tea with his mam and I'd go over to his. We were big mates and we ended up serving together right through the war. "

Ron received confirmation of his acceptance into the Army a few days after the medical. The letter also included a train ticket and informed him that he was to report to the 6th Field Training

Regiment, Royal Artillery, at Dalry, Scotland on the 29th January 1942. By a happy coincidence John and another of Ron's friends from New Brighton had also received orders to report to Dalry on the same date.

> *"We were to catch the train from Lime Street station in Liverpool at midnight on the 28th. My house was closest to the Mersey Ferry so I suggested that everyone meet at my house. We went off with our dads and called into the Nelson for a quick pint on the way."*

Although Ron's parents had no choice in his imminent departure it didn't make his leaving any easier. They already had Ron's older brother serving away with the Army, which meant that two of their sons might very well end up in harm's way. His mother in particular took it very badly.

> *"My mam made me promise that I'd come home safely. It was a good job that I didn't know what I was going into then, or I wouldn't have made that promise! The last thing she said to me was, 'Don't forget to put your underwear under your pillow every night,' and do you know what, I still do it even to this day! It's perfect for airing them!*
>
> *While we were standing on the platform at the station this 'Redcap' (Military Policeman) came up to me and asked me where my badge was. I told him, 'I'm not in yet mate, I'm just off to get started!' Just before we got on the train my dad gave the three of us some advice. He said, 'Don't ever volunteer for anything,' and I'll*

15

tell you what, it's the best bit of advice that I've ever had!"

As the whistles blew and the train began to pull out of the station, Ron felt a mixture of apprehension and excitement.

"I was sorry to be leaving my mam and dad but it was quite exciting too. I'd never been far before, just places like Preston, Crewe, Blackpool and Chester. This was a new adventure for me. The train took most of the night to get up to Scotland and it was just getting light when we reached Glasgow. From there we had to switch trains for Kilmarnock, then again for Dalry. The last bit, from Dalry station to the camp, we had to walk."

Once they had been admitted at the gate, and had their papers checked, they were allocated a billet. The train journey had been long and uncomfortable, and the men were eager to get some proper sleep.

They were going to need it. Basic Training would begin the next day.

Chapter Two

Basics

29th January - 12th March 1942

Dalry Camp in Ayrshire was just about as uninviting a place as anywhere in the British Isles. Situated on the west coast of Scotland, in the county of Ayrshire, Dalry stands on the banks of the Firth of Clyde, which separates the mainland from the windswept Isle of Arran, and the Kintyre peninsula.

The camp was home to 6th Field Training Regiment, Royal Artillery, one of a large number of such units in the country that had been formed by the British Army for the sole purpose of transforming civilians into soldiers.

"It was a proper camp, solid brick, not tented. The downside though was that all of the facilities were outside the barracks! The showers, washing facilities, toilets, they were all out in the fresh air! You know to be fair, we got there at the end of January and it was bloody cold, I'll tell you.

We were billeted in one of the brick barracks, with about twenty of us, the platoon, living in it. We had a bed with a straw mattress and a locker by the side for your gear. Our bombardier, which is like a corporal, lived in there with us as well to make sure that we were behaving ourselves!"

The process of turning this group of young men into soldiers began immediately. Early on the first morning the men were ordered to report to the Quartermaster's stores.

"We had to go over there to get all our gear, everything we'd need during the course of our training. We lined up as a 'section' and when it was your turn you'd be

measured up and given your denims, your BD's
(battledress) and the rest of your stuff."

The 'rest of your stuff' was a considerable amount of equipment, most of which would require polishing at every opportunity. Each recruit received two pairs of boots, a belt and anklets, BD's, denims, a steel helmet, a 'housewife', (a little cloth holdall which contained a needle, cotton, and thimble), and PT equipment. The ubiquitous Brasso and Blanco, the cleaning agents that would become so familiar to the men were not standard issue; they had the dubious pleasure of buying them.

Once they'd received their issue and had settled in, the training began in earnest.

"We were up at six o'clock every morning and the first thing you did was wash and shave, and it was cold, I'll tell you. Some of the lads hadn't even started shaving but they still had to do it whether they needed to or not!

After that we'd get dressed and go for a run for a couple of miles - the whole section. I was lucky; I was a fit lad, but some of the other lads really struggled and they'd have the bombardier shouting at them the whole way.

Then when we got back to our barracks we had to make our beds quickly, and you had to do a proper job, and then go straight to the mess hall for breakfast."

Running around the camp perimeter on those icy cold February mornings ensured the recruits were ravenous by the time they reached the mess hall, but for Ron it was a question of taste!

"The food was OK, to be fair; it was just the menu that wasn't my thing. Even though my dad was a Manx man I absolutely HATED kippers! I couldn't abide them, and we used to have them two or three times a week!

We used to have porridge a lot as well, which I liked, but they used to serve it with salt instead of sugar, so I couldn't eat that either! Mind you, I'd still get my portion and try and swap it with someone for a piece of bread or something."

For the recruits at Dalry, the six weeks spent there would be routine followed by more routine. The daily timetable altered very little and this made the already punishing schedule even more difficult. Straight after breakfast the men were out on the parade ground in their denims for marching and rifle drill, or MRD. This particular activity required co-ordination and a great deal of concentration. Rain and shine the men stamped around the square, honing their skills and trying hard, sometimes in vain, not to incur the wrath of the ever-watchful sergeant.

Physical Training was also a priority. If the men were going to war they would need to be ready, physically and mentally.

"Fitness training took up a lot of the time. We'd be out on the yard doing exercises, or very often we'd go on long runs in full kit, which was hard going. We also did a lot of unarmed combat, learning how to bring a man down with your bare hands.

20

We were at it day-in, day-out, and it was tough. Some lads really struggled, they just couldn't stick it and a few of them disappeared. Like I said earlier, I was very fit even before I went in the Army. I used to have a mate who trained whippets, and I used to go with him when he took them out. We used to go down onto the waterfront and I used run off a couple of hundred yards ahead waving a hanky. He'd wait until I'd gone far enough and then he'd let the dogs go to try to catch me!"

The first few weeks at Dalry were a constant round of exercise, kit inspections, marching and drilling, and being told very loudly what to do and when to do it. It took its toll on the recruits.

"It was very different from anything else I'd been used to, that's for sure! I suppose I got a bit homesick sometimes, but to be honest I was with a good bunch of lads, so that didn't really bother me much.

There was one lad there, a Scottish lad, who absolutely hated every second of it. He was a terror! He was always in trouble and after a couple of weeks we didn't see him again. He either went AWOL or they chucked him out. They couldn't do anything with him."

Saturday mornings were for kit inspection, an affair particularly hated by the men, who nonetheless prepared for it as though their lives depended on it, as the consequences of failure were too horrible to contemplate.

"Everything had to be 'spic and span', or you were for

21

it! The bombardier would walk around the room with all of us standing to attention at the end of our beds, which had to be perfectly made, with all the blankets folded properly. Your uniform had to be pressed sharply and your belts, buttons, and buckles, had to be polished and 'blancoed'.

Even the soles of your boots had to be polished! There were a few ways to get a really good shine on your boots and when I was in the Home Guard my Uncle Jack had showed me the way that he used to do his. He used to get a rib bone from the butchers and burn it slightly, then rub it into the leather. After that he'd use a cloth to finish it off with. It used to bring them up a treat!"

As the training progressed the men were allowed to spend some evenings off camp, on the condition they were back by midnight. For Ron one night was particularly memorable. He had known for some time his brother Fred was stationed nearby in Ayr with his unit, the Duke of Cornwall's Light Infantry, and after making some enquiries they got the chance meet up.

"It was great to see him. We went ice-skating that night in the town, but I hadn't been before so I spent more time on my backside than anything else! We had a great time. I met him three times altogether throughout the war, which was amazing really.

The good thing was, we didn't have to do guard duty at Dalry because the regiment that ran the camp were responsible for that. So long as we weren't on detail for anything else, we could do, as we liked. Most of the boys would go into Dalry. It was only a small place but it had a couple of cinemas, the Roxy and the Regal I think they were called.

We used to take local girls from the town. A message used to appear on the screen saying, 'Please refrain from smoking, as the smoke obscures the screen.' I remember as well that you had to pay extra to sit in the balcony, but it was only two or three steps higher than the other seats!

It was very important that we were dressed properly before we left camp. There was a mirror in the guard room and you had to stand in front of it to make sure you looked smart before the sentry would let you out."

Spending time away from the camp helped the men relax and forget the rigours of the tough regime, but sometimes even a few innocent hours in one of the town's pubs could lead to trouble.

"It was high jinks more than anything. We'd come back from the pub one night, a few of us, and someone had started a pillow fight in the barracks and it got a bit out of hand! We must have been making a hell of a racket and when the bombardier burst in, everybody managed to get into bed except me and two other lads. We got seven days C.B. for that.

On C.B. you have punishment duties. We spent the next week up to our knees in the stream that ran past the camp, taking stones out of it ONE by ONE! We did that all day long every day. In the evenings we were allowed to go to the canteen for half-an-hour. After about five days we'd cleared the stretch of the stream we were in and we went to tell the bombardier that we'd finished. All he said to us was, 'Oh, have you? Good. Now go and put them all back again, ONE by ONE!'

And we had to, one at a time."

That incident wasn't the only time that Ron fell foul of army regulations and once again the prescribed punishment was monotonous and pointless, just as it was intended to be.

"Anytime you misbehaved or messed up on the parade ground you'd end up doing something horrible. One time, I had to shovel coal from one corner of a room to the other, then sweep it out and shovel it all back again!

There were these things we called 'byngs', huge mounds of coal that were stacked in the area from the old coalface, all around the camp. We were made to run up them in full kit if we did something wrong. The bombardiers were very callous, and I suppose they had to be. They'd look you in the eye and say, 'You might have broken your mother's heart but you won't break mine!' To be fair, when we were off duty in the pub or something they were alright."

Over the first few weeks Ron had not had a lot of time to think

about home, but his mother, back in Wallasey, had not forgotten
him.

*"Up the hill from the camp there was a big blockhouse
where the 'Black Watch' were billeted, and outside
there was a 'phone box. The first time I'd rung my
mam I'd given her the number, so after that she used
to ring me at an arranged time from the butcher's
down the road from our house. My mate Ron, who'd
lost his mother, used to come with me, and my mam
used to chat to us both and keep us going, like only a
mother can!*

*Another bit of a home comfort was the big house
across the road from the camp. The family that owned
it were very wealthy but very nice to us. They didn't
find the camp an annoyance at all, and they used to
have us over in groups on a Sunday afternoon for tea."*

A couple of weeks before the end of basic training the men
began to receive weapons tuition.

*"The .303 was the rifle. We had to go to the armoury
to take our rifles out and when we'd finished practice
we took them back again. In groups we were shown
how to strip it, clean it, load it, fire it - everything. The
rifle range at the camp was round the back of the
'byngs'. I wasn't a bad shot. I used to hit the target
every now and then!*

*We learned all sorts, bayonet practice, how to prime
and throw grenades, the ' ins and outs' of the Bren gun,*

25

although I never fired the Bren during training. When that's all you're doing, all day every day, you get the hang of it. By the end of the training I think we were pretty capable."

As it was wartime the men would not undertake a passing out parade. They would shortly be leaving the camp for their first posting and despite the hardships he had endured during the training Ron knew that the time at Dalry had done him good.

"I've always said that I went into the Army a boy, tied to my mother's apron strings, but when I came out I was a man. It makes you stand up for yourself."

The only thing that remained was for Ron to find out to which unit he'd been posted. After scanning the lists on the camp notice board he was delighted to discover that he and John Mason would shortly be leaving Scotland for the southeast coast of England. They had been posted to the 86th Field Regiment, Royal Artillery.

'Gunner Kaye.' It had a nice ring to it.

Ron's father Percy,
in WWI uniform

Ron's mother Mary,
and sister Dot

Ron's brothers,
Fred (with glasses) and Les

Ron, circa 1939

Ron in Home Guard attire

Ron in Wallasey, 1946

Fred in Gibraltar, 1941

Ron during Basic Training
at Dalry, March 1942

Chapter Three

Learning Curve

13th March – May 1944

On the day of departure from Dalry, the men, after saying their good-byes, went their separate ways. They had been posted to a diversity of units the length and breadth of the country, but once again Ron and John Mason had managed to stay together. After the sometimes-insufferable hardships of Dalry Camp they now had seven days of 'leave' to look forward to, and they were going to make the most of it! Travelling back by train, they were looking forward to seeing home and the familiar faces of the community again.

"It was nice to get home to see everyone. I remember one night there was quite a bad air raid. Wallasey got hit hard, not as bad as during the Blitz, mind you, but bad enough. It was potluck. We were just lucky the time our house got hit."

Ron made the most of his leave but all too soon it was time to gather his kit, and say goodbye to his family and friends. On a crisp spring morning in the third week of March he said goodbye to his loved ones and joined his pal John Mason as they set off for Lime Street Station where they would take the train south to join their new regiment, which was currently deployed along the south east coast in support of units of 212 Infantry Brigade. At the time there was still the risk of a German invasion, and Britain was in a high state of readiness against any such attack.

The time spent at Dalry had changed Ron. He had endured and overcome mental and physical challenges that in the past he would have thought beyond him. Although this had given him new confidence and maturity, he knew he had only learned the fundamentals of soldiering and that there would be many more challenges ahead. His spirit of adventure however, ensured he was looking forward to his new posting, and any trials it would bring.

At the time, the Royal Regiment of Artillery was in an ongoing state of change. There was a critical shortage of equipment during the early years of the war as the majority of Britain's artillery, especially anti-tank guns, had been wrecked or abandoned on the beaches at Dunkirk in Northern France during the battle there in May 1940.

As well as artillery, a huge quantity of other types of equipment was lost. By early 1942, however, things had improved a lot.

All three batteries of 86th Field Regiment had received their full complement of eight 25-pounder guns, with their ammunition limbers and four-wheel drive 'Quad' towing vehicles. At the same time a new commanding officer, Lt.-Col. GD Fanshawe, who would eventually lead the regiment into battle, was posted in. He had served with the regiment, as adjutant, before the war and there were many who remembered his high standards. Life would never be easy under Colonel Fanshawe!

With a dedicated officer in command, and good quality equipment now available, the outlook was brighter for the regiment, and it was soon undertaking manoeuvres in the wide-open spaces around Salisbury Plain, and Brecon in South Wales. The new recruits were in for a busy time.

On reaching Regimental HQ in Saxmundham, in Suffolk, Ron reported for duty.

"Well, we got to the camp, there was quite a few of us like, and we were given billets and the chance to sort ourselves out. Then for the next couple of days we were in the classroom, doing tests, arithmetic and things, so that they could evaluate us. When that was over we were given our postings. I was sent to 342 Battery, C Troop, No .3 Gun. I was lucky again because John was posted to 342 as well, except that he went to D Troop. It was great because being in the same battery meant that we'd still be able to see plenty of each other."

On receiving their postings Ron and the other new members of the regiment shuffled off the parade ground and reported for duty to their new sergeants. By design, the detachment of No. 3 Gun, like all the others, had been assembled carefully with a blend of youth and experience in mind.

"The Sergeant Major was Cooper. He was great, very strict but fair and 'one of the boys'. There was another couple of sergeants too. One was Sergeant Benny Lynch; he was a dapper type with a Don Juan moustache. I didn't really have much to do with him. The other one was Sergeant Dixon; he was in charge of Number 3 Gun. He was all right, but he could be a bit smug, you know, 'I'm a sergeant, you're not', kind of thing. Those three were experienced; they'd been in the artillery since before the war. The rest of us were rookies.

There was Peter Hughes from Edinburgh, who was bloody whippets mad! There was Jock McCartney, another Scot; he was from Glasgow. Then there was Small; he was the official driver and in charge of the maintenance and logbook for our quad, the vehicle which towed the gun.

There was Jack Speed, who drove the tracked carrier, what we called the 'monkey truck'. He was a great fellow. Do you know, he used to write home every day! Then there was Clegg; he used to like 'laying the gun'. There were a lot of other lads too, but that was our gun crew, a great bunch.

On top of that, although you've only got four guns in the troop, there's a hell of a lot more people involved than just the six to each gun, because just to keep 342 Battery going it took all sorts. You've got men for the ammunition lorry, wireless operators, half-track men, 15-cwt lorry men; they'd follow the guns around with all the rations and stuff in.

Then there were the 3-ton lorry men, the carrier men; there were four or five blokes just in that. On top of all that there's the sergeants, signallers, fitters, mechanics, storemen, and all the officers. All that just for one battery."

Although Ron was more than happy with the detachment he had been assigned to, and was getting on well, there were some difficult times at the beginning.

"It was pretty obvious at the start that some officers didn't want us around. You know, we were just a bunch

of scots and scousers; rough and ready really, and we were up against a lot of snobbery. In the beginning they basically just blanked us, only bothering with us when they had to. It took quite a while before we felt a bit more accepted."

To begin with the men were tutored in the basics of artillery operations and were expected to learn the 'ins and outs' of their weapon. The 25-pdr was borne out of the British Army's need for a weapon that would include the best features of the 18-pdr field gun, and a howitzer, (a gun that fires indirectly at its target). The reasons for this were many. The 18-pdr was a very good weapon but was best suited for firing on a flat trajectory, and the Army felt that a more flexible weapon with a heavier shell was needed. A rigorous program of research, development and testing was launched.

The resulting weapon, the 25pdr gun-howitzer, became one of the most impressive field guns of its day. The flexibility of the gun made it very effective in a variety of roles. It could lob shells at targets over hills and woods at ranges of up to seven miles, or be used in an anti-tank role, where its heavy shell made it a potent weapon. It quickly won the confidence of the gunners with its ease of use and its effectiveness, and by the time Ron joined the regiment, the 25-pdr was firmly established as the mainstay of British field artillery.

"The first gun I trained with was the 25-pdr, the old quad, limber and gun set-up. The quad was the truck. The limber, where the ammunition was stored, was

hooked up to the back of it, with the gun towed behind that. We started training straight away. There was a process that we had to learn and we practised and practised it until we could do it almost without thinking. We'd be riding along in the quad and when the order came we had to stop straight away. Then it was all about speed. We were practising for war so we took it very seriously.

After the quad had stopped, the sergeant would detail a couple of men to unhook the limber and another couple to unhook the gun. Then we had to get set up as quickly as possible. There was a turntable underneath the gun and when you pulled two handles down at the side, the turntable dropped to the floor so that the gun could traverse on it. To stop the gun moving when it was fired there was a brake lever.

As soon as we were ready the No.3 in the crew would 'lay the gun', which was quite technical but basically means to aim it. Between shots the gun would be checked to make sure it hadn't moved. There would be blokes up ahead of you setting tannoys up, which relayed the instructions back to us at the gun from whoever was in the O.P., the observation post.

We might have to fire miles ahead, which the 25-pdr was well capable of, so you'd need someone spotting for you and letting you know things like, the elevation you needed, the type of shell required, what the target was, all sorts.

That information would come back by wireless to our command post up ahead where an officer would relay it to us over the tannoys. At our end, the 'gun end', the Gun Position Officer or GPO, would then give us the orders. He might order four rounds a minute, or any other combination.

As gunners we wouldn't be involved in the drawing up of the 'fire-plan'; only officers got involved in that side of things. We were responsible for getting the shells ready, and firing. The shells were stored in fours in the limber along with the cartridge cases.

Once you'd opened the breech of the gun and rammed the shell in, you then put the cartridge case in with whichever type of cordite you needed - charge 1,2, or 3. The cordite came in little coloured bags and you added or removed some of them depending on the range of the target.

We learned how to prime the shell, and which fuses to use in different situations. The cartridge cases had three charges; red, white, and blue, and the officer in the OP would send a message back telling you which one you needed to use.

There were different types for elevations and distances. The type of shell was colour coded too. High Explosive, (HE), was brown; Armour Piercing, (AP), was black, and Smoke was green. There was a lot to it but we trained hard and we got the hang of it pretty well in the end."

In June 1942, shortly after Ron's arrival, the 86th was transferred from the 54th Infantry Division to the 42nd Armoured Division, as one of the two regiments of the divisional artillery. At the same time orders were received informing the regiment that it was on the move, this time to Slingsby, in Yorkshire. The reason for this move became apparent shortly after the unit arrived at its new home. The Yorkshire Moors, with its wide-open spaces, were perfect 'tank country'; ideal for the 42rd Division's armour and mechanised infantry battalions to train on.

For the 86th, this type of training was rather different from what it had become used to down south, where it had been deployed in a static defensive role, but hard training ensured that it adjusted to its new role quickly.

"The training up there was hard going, but we had some fun too. Some of the regiment were billeted in Nissen huts in a village called Hovingham, but we were in Slingsby. It was only a small place, near Malton. There was an old ruined castle next to the camp and one night, when my mate John Leiper was on guard duty, a few of the lads in the troop jumped out on him with white sheets over their heads! He nearly jumped out of his skin! Poor old John; he was killed in action later on in the war, in France.

The thing that I remember most, though, about Slingsby Camp was the guardroom. It was absolutely crawling with earwigs, and I couldn't bear blasted earwigs. It was so bad that none of the lads would go in there. When we were on guard duty we used to stand outside on the running boards of vehicles instead!"

All through the summer and autumn of 1942, the training continued.

"We were doing all sorts and it was paying off because we were getting very good at our job. Even though we were an artillery regiment we were doing a lot of training with other types of weapons as well; rifles, pistols, Bren guns, etc.

You had to know every job on the 25-pdr too. We all had our own job but we trained to know each others because in combat someone might get killed or injured, so it was important that we could fill in for each other if need be. I liked being the No.2 if I had a choice; shoving the shell into the breech of the gun; I used to love doing that!"

During the time at Slingsby, the regiment spent a lot of time at nearby Spaunton Moor firing range, where 'dry' exercises (with no ammunition), and 'live firing' both took place. Later when the unit was training around the Whitby Bay area, firing out to sea, the 'powers that be' provided the men with some novel target practice.

"You'll never believe this, but at Whitby we were firing out to sea at a target towed by an aeroplane! I thought at the time, 'you're chancing your luck mate!"

After six months of intensive training in Yorkshire the regiment was ordered to move into winter billets in nearby Scarborough. It was very welcome news after the tough regime at Slingsby.

"Everyone was trying to get a billet in one of the guest houses on the sea front, and I was one of the lucky ones. We'd been sent to Scarborough for the winter and for a wireless course, Morse code and that, but to be honest, I only went for the hell of it!

I was billeted in a two-room place and I was sharing with another 'scouse' lad, I forget his name now. Anyway, there was a little sink in the corner of the room and one morning after this lad had washed his hair, it all fell out, eyebrows everything! He'd picked up some disease, and off he went to the M.O. (Medical Officer).

The next time we saw him was in Germany about two and a half years later, near the end of the war! His hair had begun to grow back; he had little tufts all over his head. He looked like a Red Indian! He'd been determined to rejoin the regiment.

At Scarborough I got into another scrape and was given seven days CB again. I thought to myself, 'Oh no, I'm not going to have to pick all the stones off Scarborough Beach, am I?' My mind went back to Dalry! I failed the wireless course as well!"

Christmas came and went, and at the end of February 1943, after completing a two-week exercise in Northamptonshire, which involved capturing a bridge and executing a fighting withdrawal, the regiment moved again. The destination this time was Upton Lovell Camp, near Codford in Wiltshire. The stay was brief, especially for 341 and 342 Batteries, but it was while the 86th was stationed there that a very significant event occurred. The regiment learned that it was to become a self-propelled unit.

The idea of self-propelled artillery had been around for some time. In the late 1930's Germany had been quick to acknowledge the important role that this type of weapon would play in the new, mobile era of warfare, and later on used it to great effect in the Blitzkrieg operations against Poland, France and Russia. Other nations around the globe were also experimenting with S.P. artillery, and in 1942/3 the 86th Field Regiment was allocated Britain's version, the hastily designed Bishop, a Valentine tank chassis married with a 25-pdr gun.

The events surrounding the 86th's introduction to its new guns are the subject of many debates, but at the time the C.O., Lt. Col. Fanshawe made the following entry in his diary.

"One day (20th March) I had a message from the station master that 24 tanks had arrived by train, addressed to the regiment, and would I please send someone to take them over. Not unnaturally, we thought a mistake had been made, as no warning or notification had been received by anyone. However, it was found that they were intended for us and were self-propelled guns. Fortunately we had recently had a subaltern posted to us who had been in a tank regiment, so he went down to the station, only a few hundred yards away, and drove all 24 guns to the camp; and so the Herts Yeomanry were the first, or almost the first, field regiment to become self-propelled."

Over the years various people who claim to have been eyewitnesses have contradicted Fanshawe's version of events, as well as each other. Some have said that it took a full week to get all of the Bishops to the camp, and some have said it took only two days. Whatever the truth, the task was somehow completed and that training with these 'new fangled' machines began immediately. Within days the regiment had undertaken 'live firing' practice.

"It was a big change but to be honest we enjoyed it. It was something new; it felt a bit more enterprising. We felt like it was a big change, but a good change. Mind you, it was very different to the Q.L.G. We were used to a lot of running around, but with the S.P. it was just a case of firing and throwing the empty cartridge case over the side! The end result was the same because although we were now mobile in our own right, being on the tank, we were still using a 25-pdr gun.

The big plus for me was that you felt that much more confident with the S.P. around you. All that steel made you feel more secure even though there was no roof on it! With the Q.L.G. you were always out in the open and totally exposed to the enemy, even though we never used it in action. We did a lot of practising on Salisbury Plain and we soon got the hang of it."

Indeed, training progressed well enough over the weeks leading up to the end of May for Lt. Col. Fanshawe to report to his superiors that the 86th was 'up and running' as a self propelled field regiment. Hard work, teamwork, and dedication had made it possible, but despite this, the most important question, as far as the men of the batteries were concerned, remained unanswered. Why had the 86th become a 'self propelled' regiment?

They were about to find out.

Chapter Four

Countdown to D-Day

May 1943 – June 1944

Ever since they had been vanquished from France in May 1940, the problem of how and when they could attempt a return remained uppermost in the minds of the Allies. By the spring of 1943 Britain's fortunes were in stark contrast to the perilous position it had found itself in approximately two years earlier. Then, woefully short of vital equipment, it had stood alone against the tyranny of Nazi Germany.

Now, things were different. Events had shown that Adolf Hitler's forces were not unbeatable. General Montgomery and his famous 'Desert Rats' had won a convincing victory in the North African desert, and in the east the Russians had destroyed an entire German army, the 6th, in and around the shattered remains of the city on the Volga, Stalingrad. Further, the United States had joined the conflict after the unprovoked Japanese attack on its Pacific fleet at Pearl Harbour in 1941, and after two years of savage fighting the U.S. had struck a decisive blow in the campaign against the Japanese, with a telling naval victory around the island of Midway.

Despite these successes the price had been high, especially for the Russians. In attempting to hold the Germans the country had suffered terribly. Millions of soldiers and civilians had become casualties in a conflict that was by design, 'a war of extermination'. The Russian premier, Josef Stalin, was growing increasingly impatient with what he saw as Britain and America's unwillingness to open a 'second front' in the West, an event which he believed would reduce the pressure on his beleaguered troops and force the Germans into their nightmare scenario - a war on two fronts.

In reality, Churchill and Roosevelt, the leaders of Britain and America respectively, more than realised the need for a return to the European mainland, and had agreed a policy of 'Germany first', quite rightly identifying that country as the most dangerous of the Axis powers.

It would not be easy. Launching a successful assault against 'Fortress Europe' would require enormous amounts of highly trained manpower, specialised equipment, and complex planning; all of which would take a substantial amount of time to generate. In fact, the build-up had already started. America's entry into the war had seen them bring their huge manufacturing potential to the Allied cause. Tanks, aeroplanes, ships, weapons, equipment of every sort, were being mass-produced 24 hours a day in the U.S., far from where the German bombers could interfere with them. On top of this, the U.S. had been steadily shipping troops to Britain since as early as January 1942, and over the next three years over 1.5 million G.I.s. would use Britain as a 'stepping stone' to the European battlefields.

To appease Stalin while the main event was being prepared, and to glean vital information necessary for future planning, it was decided that ' a reconnaissance in force' would be sent to test the mettle of the German coastal defences in Northern France. The raid, Operation Jubilee, took place in August 1942 with near disastrous results. The 2nd Canadian Infantry Division, along with some British Commandos and American Rangers, attacked along a 16-kilometre front around the French port of Dieppe and were beaten back with heavy losses. Of the approximate 6,000 troops involved more than half became casualties, or prisoners of war.

Terrible though the outcome was, the raid provided an invaluable insight into the problems of large-scale amphibious landings. After full-scale debriefings and analysis of the assault, the Allies were able to form the basic plan of what would become Operation Overlord, the Allied invasion of Europe.

Dieppe had shown that large-scale naval and air support would be vital to any future landings, but there was one other aspect that had been viewed as crucial to a successful assault - the need for tanks to land on the beaches ahead of the infantry so that when they deployed, they would have immediate armoured support.

Further, another highly innovative notion was suggested, and it was particularly relevant to the 86th Field Regiment. Would it be possible to arrange the self-propelled artillery in such a way on the landing craft that they could accurately bombard the shore defences on the 'run-in' to the beach?

It was an intriguing idea - and at the very least, worthy of a trial. At the beginning of May 1943, 341 and 342 batteries of the 86th Field Regiment left Wiltshire and travelled down to Blandford, Dorset. On arrival in the area the purpose of the move was revealed as 'for training in beach landings'. The phrasing of the words left little doubt in the men's minds. This was the first clue to any future role that the unit would play, although there was still no hint as to when or even where it would be sent.

For the batteries at Blandford this was a bit of a 'feather in their cap'. Although in the coming September Allied landings would take place in Sicily and the Italian mainland, these assaults would not be using self-propelled artillery to bombard the shore during their approach to the beach. Consequently, it had not been deemed necessary for training of this type to be undertaken, and as a result the 86th had been chosen to all intents and purposes, to write the book on this manner of assault.

It was unknown territory. It had not been tried before, and the men knew that laying down accurate fire from a landing craft to the shore in potentially heavy seas would not be easy. Further, attacking a heavily fortified coastline would inevitably mean that they themselves would be under fire. This, and a multitude of other problems, would have to be mastered if the assignment was to be successful.

Starting from scratch the batteries set about their task. Due to the security precautions surrounding the 'second front' planning, the batteries at Blandford were told precious little about the task they were undertaking, but they knew it was important. The Army had very wisely provided the batteries with the specifications of the vessels, the Landing Craft Tank, (LCT), that would be used to transport the regiment to any future combat zone. In this way the vessels could be marked out on the ground and practised on.

The Landing Craft Tank (LCT), a large, no-frills vessel was capable of carrying six medium tanks on its deck space. Further, due to the design of its hull it could then deploy the vehicles through its drop-down front in very shallow water, making it a vital piece of equipment for any amphibious assault. The 86th however, also had a number of support vehicles for each troop' and the initial period at Blandford was spent working out how best to load all of the regiment's equipment into the craft. This initial stage, 'loading training', was very important and over the next few weeks the men worked very hard with their version of the LCTs.

There were a number of important considerations regarding this aspect of the training. It would be vital for the self propelled guns to have enough space on the LCTs so that they would be able to operate effectively, and further, they would need to be able to disembark quickly upon landing. These necessities had to be weighed up against physical space on the crafts' decks, and after weeks of toil and perseverance it was determined that each of the six troops which made up the 86th, would need an LCT of its own.

By mid-July, the batteries were ready to begin 'live firing' practice, for which they moved to Studland Bay, near Poole in Dorset. This was a critical phase of the operation; the 86th would have roughly a month to perfect the art of firing 'ship to shore', which did not leave a great deal of margin for error. Co-operation and co-ordination between the naval and army contingents would have to be total if the necessary blueprint was to be produced, especially between the gun position officers, (GPOs), and the officers of the LCTs, because it was this relationship that would establish the direction in which the shells would leave the barrels of the 25-pdrs as they closed with the shoreline.

For the month up to the middle of August, Studland Bay was

full of activity as the regiment and their naval colleagues worked on 'getting it right'. A suggestion to group all six LCTs in a tight formation, with a radar motor-boat alongside to help them maintain course, was tried and quickly adopted, and slowly but surely the plan was whittled into shape. At the end of the training in the third week of August the regimental report was very upbeat in its analysis of the past month's activity when it noted:

> '(The exercise) proved to everybody's satisfaction that a self-propelled regiment carried in six LCTs, could produce a concentration of fire covering an area 300 yards square under the worst weather conditions in which an invasion could be carried out.'

It wasn't just the official report that noted the success of the exercise; the men themselves were pleased, too.

> *"Well, we'd worked very hard and it had paid off. It went smoothly and it was very successful. We were confident; we knew we could do this now. Mind you, while we were down there we still had to practice survival techniques in case anything went wrong. Things like getting out of the sea with all your kit on.*
>
> *That was the thing I hated most about all of the training; wherever we went we always seemed to be cold and wet! While we were in Wiltshire, sometimes on a Saturday morning, we'd be taken in trucks to the middle of nowhere on Salisbury Plain and left there to find our own way back to camp. The flaps would be down on the lorry so we couldn't memorise the routes,*

and we'd have a map and a compass with us, and that
was all!

In groups of four or five we'd set off back to camp.
Once you were back the day was your own, so
everyone was keen to get back as fast as possible.
Sometimes it would be pouring with rain and the wind
would be howling but God help you if you were caught
hitching a lift! A lot of the time we'd get back, and
we'd be soaked to the skin."

Now that the experiment in Poole had been completed
successfully, 341 and 342 batteries travelled north to
Kilmarnock in Scotland to join their sister battery, 462, where it
too had been practising. As the year had worn on the training
schedule had been getting more hectic and gruelling by the day,
because although no date had yet been set for the 'second front',
everyone knew that it would come at some point in the not too
distant future, and that they would need to be ready.

"We were off everywhere; all over the place. We spent
quite a lot of time in Scotland, in places like Kilbride
Bay, the Isle of Arran, and at Inverary, which no one
was supposed to know about. Everywhere we'd been
we'd had a good social life. We'd always been treated
well by the locals wherever we were, but Scotland was
the best, they really took to us up there.

I can remember one time I was going on leave to see
my sister, but my train didn't leave until midnight so
I called into a pub in Kilmarnock for a couple of pints

first. I went up to the bar and asked for a pint of 'mix'
which where I come from is half bitter and half mild.
Well I soon found out that up there it was half bitter
and half red wine! Anyway, I got chatting to this bloke
and I told him that I had to hang around until midnight
for my train. Do you know what? He took me back to
his house and his wife cooked me a meal and then later
on this fellow gave me a lift back to the station. The
hospitality was brilliant up there."

As the winter of 1943 moved in, the regiment said goodbye to
Scotland and returned south, first to Suffolk, and then in
December into winter accommodation in Norwich, which is still
vivid in Ron's mind for a very painful reason.

"We were down there for a bit of a rest but we still had
stuff to do. I remember that John and I had arranged
a date with a couple of local girls; we were off to the
cinema in the evening, but when the time came to meet
up with them I was still stuck on camp in some
classroom lecture. As time went on I was getting more
and more anxious because I knew that John had
already left to meet up with the girls.

As soon as we were finished I scurried out of the room and
shot off to meet John at the cinema. It was winter so it was
already dark, and as I was chasing around a street corner
I ran smack-bang into a lamppost! Well that was it for me!
It knocked me clean out and off to Thorpe Hospital I went
with concussion. Two weeks I was in there."

Christmas and the New-Year came and went, and were celebrated in the traditional army fashion. At the beginning of February 1944 the 86th once again received new guns. The US-made 105mm Priests, which had replaced the Bishop in August 1943, were discarded and in their place came the Sextons. Although the men didn't know it yet, these were the guns they would take into battle.

Although the Priest had been an excellent weapon, there was one fundamental problem with it as far as the British were concerned, and that was the calibre of its gun. 105mm was not a standard British calibre and therefore supply of shells was always a problem. To remedy this, the British suggested that the Priest chassis be fitted with a 25-pdr gun, but the Americans withdrew from the idea, as they didn't want to mass-produce a weapon they had no intention of adopting as a standard U.S. weapon. As a result the British looked elsewhere, and soon came up with the idea of combining the chassis of the Canadian Ram tank with the standard British 25-pdr artillery piece.

The result was the Sexton. Twenty feet long, nine feet wide, over eight feet high, and weighing nearly twenty-six tons, it was an imposing sight. Its nine-cylinder engine was surrounded by armour 112mm thick and allowed the Sexton to travel at up to 24mph, and up to 125 miles before needing to be refuelled. As well as the main gun, the six-man crew also carried two Bren guns in the vehicle for local defence of the gun position. In short, it was a formidable weapon, and after training with it, the men of the regiment quickly came to like it.

"It was definitely the best. Everything you needed was

there with you, and the fact that you had everything to hand made up for the lack of space on board. One thing about the lack of space was that you had to be very careful with the recoil of the gun. I've seen blokes knocked about by it. You have to remember that the recoil of a 25-pdr is staggering.

It was a huge thing, about 25 tons unloaded. It wasn't as manoeuvrable as the others; the Valentine could turn on a sixpence, but it was faster than them. One thing I didn't like about it though was the 50-gallon tank of reserve petrol that was stored on the back! That, along with all the ammo that was stored under your feet made it a bit of a bomb if you got hit.

It was open-topped, obviously, so later on in the war we had steel rails welded on to the sides in an arch shape, so that we could put canvas over them for a bit of protection from the wind and rain. We also had rods welded onto the front so that we could carry spare parts for the tracks, or whatever. We used to like them because we thought that they might give us a bit more protection from enemy tanks."

During February of 1944, as the troops got to grips with their Sextons, the 86th learned that it was to be transferred from the 49th Division to the very experienced 50th Division. Although they weren't told as much, the reason for this move was simple; it had now been decided that the 49th Division would take no part in the actual assault. The battle-hardened 50th Division though, with its experience in the North African and Italian campaigns, would play a key role.

When the men of 50th Division discovered that they had been chosen again, they were justifiably angry, arguing that they had 'done their bit'. The practical reasons for selecting the division though were sound; experience would be vital in the assault and the 50th had as much as any other formation in the British Army.

The Allied High Command was taking no chances with the invasion plan, knowing full well that failure was not an option. If the Germans could stop the invasion in its infancy the war in Europe could well be lost. By defeating the Allies in the west, they would then be in a position to transfer many of their divisions to the Eastern Front, which could tip the balance of that conflict back into Germany's favour. The invasion must succeed; that was the doctrine, and for this to happen the Allies were assembling an awesome fighting force.

Operation Overlord, the Allied invasion of Europe, was, and still is the largest and most complex sea borne assault ever undertaken. In broad terms the Allies were attempting to deploy a sizeable force to capture and hold a section of the French coastline. Once a foothold had been achieved further forces could be brought ashore and the campaign to liberate Western Europe could commence.

Where?

When the location for the assault was being considered General Eisenhower, the Supreme Commander, had to consider a number of crucial factors. The invasion site would need to be not too heavily defended, be within range for the fighters that would provide vital air cover, and be near a port that could be captured from the rear and made operational quickly. Further, the beaches themselves would need to be wide and flat with firm sand, which would allow large scale unloading direct from the supply ships possible. Adequate exits leading off the beaches, linked to a good road network for quick movement inland were another priority.

Although there was a myriad of other considerations regarding the prospective site, these were the ones that could not be compromised. After painstaking examination many areas met some of the criteria listed above but were deemed unsuitable for one reason or another. The Pas-de-Calais, with its proximity to Britain and direct route to the industrial heartland of Germany was the favoured site, except that for those very reasons it was also the most heavily defended. Here, Hitler's 'Atlantic Wall' was closer to reality than anywhere else. Enormous guns and high-quality troops would ensure that any landing in the area would almost certainly lead to disaster.

With the Pas-de-Calais out of the frame, the elimination process eventually led to a 50-mile stretch of the Normandy coastline being selected. Not only was it suitable, but the prospective landing beaches would be protected from the worst of the Atlantic weather by the Cherbourg peninsula.

When?

With the location chosen the next question was, when could the invasion be launched? Once again certain conditions would be necessary. The weather would need to be moderately calm, the moon at least half-full, and the tide low and rising so that the deadly beach obstacles would be visible. Also nothing could happen until at least the beginning of June, as the required amount of landing craft wouldn't be available until then.

When all of this had been weighed-up, after months of discussion, debate, and no shortage of arguing between the commanders planning the assault, the final plan was agreed upon; D-Day would be June 5th 1944, with H-Hour at dawn.

The Plan

In the initial assault five divisions, two American, two British, and one Canadian, would attempt to land over a 50-mile front. The U.S. forces would land in the west around the Carentan Estuary at beaches code-named Utah and Omaha, and the British and Canadians would come ashore further east between Port-en-Bessin and Ouistreham, on beaches designated Gold, Juno, and Sword.

Further, during the night before the seaborne assault, three airborne divisions would be dropped to secure the flanks of the invasion site. The American 82nd and 101st would seal off the west flank, and the 6th British, the east, and a strong moon would be necessary; to allow the paratroopers and glider men to execute their tasks with sufficient light. Backing up the assault force would be a vast armada of sea power, which would not only provide vital fire support for the ground assault, but would also transfer vast amounts of troops, supplies and equipment, as the battle unfolded.

Further, by this point of the war, Allied air superiority was complete. Prior to the assault thousands of tons of bombs would be dropped onto the fortifications around the beaches and the railway lines of the interior, which would inhibit the defenders from bringing reserves, especially armour, into the battle. The outline plan was scrutinised and fine-tuned, then turned over to the divisional commanders so the detail could be added. The planners spent thousands of hours working in utmost secrecy until finally, Operation Overlord was ready. The blueprint had been laid down, and its scale dwarfed anything that had ever been attempted before.

The beach in the centre of the five, code-named Gold was where the 50th Division would attack. From Le Hamel (Asnelles) in the west, to La Riviere (Ver-sur-Mer) in the east, the assault area for Gold stretched about three miles, and had been split into two sectors by the Allied planners; Jig, on the right, (from the attackers' perspective), and King, on the left.

King Beach, in front of the La Riviere stronghold, was itself subdivided into two parts, Green and Red, and would be assaulted by the 50th Division's 69th Brigade; the formation to which the 86th Field Regiment would shortly be assigned for the operation.

To gain some idea of the scale of the Allied assault, the following is a breakdown of how the plan was designed to unfold. The expression H- or H+, followed by a number simply means whether or not the event was to occur before or after the beginning of the attack, H-Hour.

H-7 Hours: For nearly six hours RAF bombers fly 1,316 missions, dropping 5,853 tons of explosives on German shore batteries and emplacements.

H-60 Mins: US Air Force take over and drop 7,348 tons of bombs, at the same time the Naval bombardment groups commence their fire plans against the German defences.

H-15 Mins: Landing Craft Rocket (LCR) unleash 20,000 rockets onto the British beaches, while self-propelled artillery (25-pdr Sextons) start firing as they get within range of the shore.

H-5 Mins: The DD ('swimming tanks') put to sea, six miles out and engage targets as soon as they are grounded.

H-Hour: Assault engineers, who are to clear lanes in the beach obstacles for the imminent arrival of the infantry landing craft, go ashore.

H+7 Mins: Infantry deploy in two waves, followed 40 minutes later by reserve units, beach control parties, anti-tank weapons, flamethrowers and various other equipment.

H+90 Mins: Self-propelled artillery lands, followed by towed artillery and anti-tank weapons.

For such a complex operation, many formations would require specialist units attached to them, as was the case of 86th Field Regiment. With the invasion only months away the planners wished to ensure that any units joining other formations for the operation were coupled immediately, so that maximum time was allowed for training purposes. In early March of 1944 86th Field Regiment was assigned to 69th Brigade of 50th Division, and right up until D-Day it never undertook an exercise without it. Given the activity and training schedules it was becoming clear to everyone that the invasion date was looming.

At the end of March the regiment played its part in the 'Smash' exercises at Studland Bay, Poole, that were designed to be as realistic and detailed as circumstances would allow, and once again the successful outcome ensured that the troops came out of the experience confident in their ability. The 86th was now sent to its final destination before the landings took place. Camp 14, (or C-14 as the men would come to call it), near Romsey, was just one of many purpose-built sites dotted around the picturesque New Forest region, that would be home to hundreds of thousands of young men of the army while they waited for their date with destiny.

"It was when we got to Romsey that the rumours about the invasion really started. Everyone was talking about the Second Front. When were we going? Where would it be? We hadn't been told anything yet but it was pretty obvious that something was going on cos we were penned into these camps with barbed wire and fences and guards all around us. We only went off camp for training and exercises, nothing else; but John and me managed to wangle a quick trip home!

We'd been detailed to take surplus vehicles back to Shrewsbury and after we'd dropped them off we were to return to Romsey straight away, by train. Anyway, we didn't do that; we caught a train to near where we lived. See, by not going to Liverpool we could avoid the 'redcaps', the Military Police.

We knew that we'd be going abroad soon because we'd had to take our full kit with us, rifle and all, so we thought that this might be a good chance to go home 'cos to be honest we didn't know when we'd be back again. We'd have been in terrible trouble if we'd have been caught, but we weren't, and we enjoyed ourselves! We went back to camp the following day and made up some story, I forget now, and we got away with it. I remember I had a portrait done shortly after getting back."

As the days and weeks ticked away Britain, and the south of England in particular was a hive of activity. Hundreds of thousands of men, and a multitude of vehicles, aeroplanes and other equipment were crammed into every hut, field, wood and hangar available. A wag had summed it up perfectly when he warned that if the invasion didn't come soon, Britain was in danger of sinking! At Romsey final preparations were underway.

"At C-14 there was a long road running by the side of the camp and all of our tanks were parked up on the grass verge. One of the big jobs was waterproofing them. It took days! We had to put Bostik all over them, anywhere that water could get in. The exhausts all had extensions fitted so that the engine would be all right, but just in case, there was a mechanism that would blow the waterproofing off when we beached. Be fair, they'd thought of everything."

With Overlord now only a week away senior officers gave large-scale briefings but still there was no mention of the impending attack.

"We were given big sit-down talks by the officers; of course there was no mention of D-Day! It was just another 'exercise' we were doing. Nobody believed that and we knew that the countdown had started."

No one moved in or out of C-14, or any of the other camps for that matter. The façade of Overlord being 'just another exercise' didn't last long and briefings were given in all seriousness. Allied reconnaissance units had performed a remarkable job in compiling an extremely detailed dossier on the geography, topography, enemy strength, and defences of the landing beaches. Over the coming days the men were encouraged to study the maps, photographs, sand tables and models, which the research had unearthed, and the plan for each unit was reiterated endlessly. There would be no second chance.

On 3rd June, Camp 14 began to empty as the assault units, guns and vehicles began their journey to Southampton Docks for loading. At this point D-Day was still scheduled for the 5th, so everything was concentrated around that date.

"We packed up all of our gear and left the camp on the 3rd which was a Saturday. The weather must have been fairly decent because I remember we drove through Romsey and there were people sitting outside the pubs having a drink. It was torture! I could have murdered a pint!

It took quite a while to get to Southampton because of all the army traffic on the roads. If anyone had been in any doubt about the invasion they weren't after they saw Southampton Docks that day. It was an unbelievable sight! You wouldn't have been able to get another ship in there if you'd tried. A few of us were a bit apprehensive but you couldn't help feeling excited either.

Apart from the ships there were thousands and thousands of troops and sailors milling about, and God knows how many vehicles, tanks, jeeps artillery pieces, every type of equipment, being lifted by cranes onto ships or driven onto the big LSTs through their huge bow doors. There were barrage balloons, the big reels for the fuel pipeline, PLUTO, [Pipe Line Under The Ocean)] everything you can imagine. The size of the operation was indescribable, and I've never forgotten it."

It was indeed staggering. From a logistical and planning perspective Overlord was an incredible achievement. From every port and harbour available around Britain, 3,000 ships of every kind, carrying over 2,000 landing craft were ready to transport the assaulting forces to the landing sites. In the first 24-hours alone 175,000 men, 1,500 tanks, 3,000 artillery pieces, and 10,000 other vehicles would be landed, because getting ashore was only a part of the problem; the assaulting troops would need armoured support if they were to stay ashore and consolidate the beachhead.

There were further considerations. The raid at Dieppe had shown that capturing a working port would be almost impossible, so with the ingenuity that often comes from war, the Allies decided to take their own with them. In 1942 work had begun on two artificial harbours code-named Mulberries. Enormous 6,000 ton caissons of steel and concrete, combined with a line of purposely sunk old ships, code-named Gooseberries, would form a breakwater about a mile offshore in about 200 feet of the Channel water.

These barriers would provide protection for the piers inside the perimeter, which had ingeniously designed 'floating' roadways, attached to them that were linked to the shore. The Mulberries would offer a vital advantage, as the Germans would be calculating their counterattack around the premise of the Allies having to unload all of their supplies and ammunition from landing craft over the beaches themselves. The incredible achievement of constructing and fixing the Mulberries is perfectly illustrated by the fact that each one, positioned off Gold and Omaha beaches, was roughly the size of Dover harbour.

At Southampton Docks it was soon time for the 86th to begin loading. The three Troops and the rest of the regiment's personnel spent the afternoon positioning their vehicles in the prescribed fashion on board the six LCTs that they would be sailing in.

"By the time we'd got everything onto the ship you could hardly move around. Every inch of deck space

was crammed with vehicles and equipment, all chained down in case of rough seas. That's another thing that sticks in my mind, the sound of the chains 'clanking' as we were waiting to go.

Once we'd loaded it was just a case of waiting. We left for the first time on the night of the 4th, the Sunday morning, but we only got just past the Needles. The weather had taken a turn for the worse and we had orders to return to Southampton."

This was the scenario that Eisenhower and his team had dreaded. Foul weather in the Channel forced the Supreme Commander to postpone the assault for at least 24hrs. An entire invasion force cooped up on thousands of ships lay in limbo along the south coast, and now there was a possibility that the assault would not happen in the immediate future.

"When we got back to the Needles we anchored there and waited for further orders. We weren't told what was going on so we just had to wait it out, and it wasn't very pleasant! Like I've said, there wasn't much space on board once everything had been loaded, so you just had to do the best you could. I was lucky, I had good 'sea legs' but the LCT was a flat-bottomed ship and in that weather some of the lads really suffered.

It was very stuffy and hot because we were below decks and next to the engine room, so we had all the smell from the fuel and oil. It was hard to see the boys like that because some of them were so sea sick that they

*were just lying around limp on the floor, vomiting into
their helmets.*

*I'll tell you what though; I was all right for grub!
There was that many of the lads that were ill, that they
were just giving their rations away! The food tins had
methylated spirits and a wick attached to them, and
when you lit it, it warmed the food up. They were all
right."*

All night and the following day the men waited in the cramped
conditions of the LCT, while back at Southwick House in
Hampshire, General Eisenhower agonised over the biggest
decision he would ever have to make. Could the invasion be
launched in such adverse weather?

*"We had a hell of a time while we were anchored there.
It affected people in different ways; some lads were
quiet, some were trying to sleep, some were just too ill
to care, and some were just lying there saying nothing.
I think a few were just crying and to be honest I wasn't
far off myself! It was starting to hit us what we were
facing.*

*My mate Peter and I spent a lot of the time chatting
with a member of the crew, who was a 'scouser' as
well. He was very good to us, he was; he brought us
cocoa every now and again. I remember playing cards
with him and him teaching me how to get in and out of
my hammock. I spent half the time on the bloody floor!*

Another thing, which helped to pass the time, was the

65

little French phrase books that we'd all been given.
We practiced our French for a bit, learning to say
'Good morning' and 'kiss my ear hole!"

In the late evening of 4th June, despite the adverse weather, the fleet had once again been told to form up and be ready for the order to sail. A few hours later on the morning of the 5th, as the sailors and soldiers of the invasion fleet waited impatiently on their crowded vessels, General Eisenhower arrived at Southwick House for the final weather meeting, which considering the howling winds and gusting rain that morning, did not seem promising.

If the invasion had to be cancelled now it would mean returning all of these men and their equipment to the staging areas. Morale would suffer and more importantly security could be compromised. If one word reached the Germans regarding the location of the invasion, a catastrophe would ensue.

In Southwick House, Eisenhower's mood lifted a little when his chief weather forecaster, Group Captain Stagg, entered the room with a grin on his face. In his report he assured the pacing commander and his team that for a short period on the evening of the 5th and the early hours of the 6th the current storm would break and that a spell of calm weather would ensue; after that he believed that the weather would worsen again. For about a minute Eisenhower paced up and down the room, all eyes on him. Finally he stopped, and turning to his team he said quietly but clearly, 'OK, let's go.'

A cheer was followed by numerous telephoned orders to the

naval and army commanders at the ports around the country. Movement to the rendezvous point could commence as scheduled; D-Day would now be 6th June 1944.

It was on.

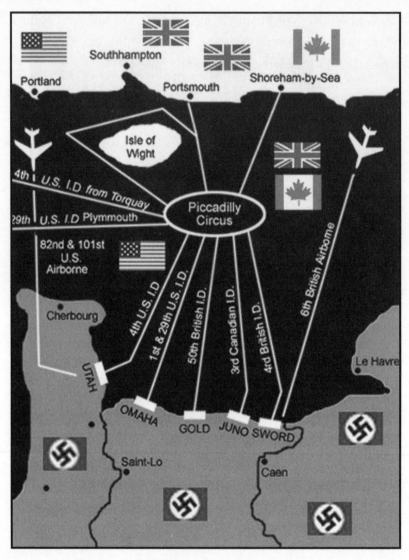

Normandy Invasion Plan

Sexton in Ver-Sur-Mer

Ron (top right) & three mates, at Codford, Wiltshire 1943

Peter from Scotland in his 'zoot suit'

John Mason, Brussells, 1944

Dusty Wellin, ammunition truck driver, 342 battery

Sgt Major Cooper

Jock McCartney

Sgt Major Dixon

Peter Hughes

MOST OF C. TROOP ROMSEY C.14. MAY 1944

Back Row - 1.Bill Wynn 2.Hartigan 3.Les Slattan 4.Peter Hughes 5.Leider 6.Jack Speed 7.Ron Kaye 8.Dennis 9.Turner
10.Sid Laws 11.Thurland 12.Thomas 14.Capsee 15.Elmer 17.Small 18.Ansel
Middle Row - 19.Ron Ager 20.Gibbons 21.G.Goard 22.Dawson 23.McCarthey 25.Russ Hobday 26.Bill Wrench 27.G.Slack
28.Alf Hart 29.Bob Carter 30.Williams 31.Copeland 33.Stanton 35.Blackerby 36.Bates
Front Row - 37.McKay 38.Andrews 39.Sgt Francis 40.Sgt Ross Stockwood 42.Lt.Mather 43. Cpt Street 44.Sgt Maj Cooper
45.Cpt Homma 46.Sgt Bill Rist 47.Sgt Dixon 48.Sgt Benny Lynch 49.Sgt Les Boasted 50.Smith 51.George Dunham
52.Bdr Bill Bottom

72

Chapter Five

Day of Destiny

6th June 1944

By June of 1944 the people of Normandy had been living under Nazi rule for a little over four years. In every village and town the people had long become accustomed to curfews, checkpoints, roadblocks, and the indignity of having to carry identity papers on their own home soil.

The fifth of June, a Monday, was much like any other day of the occupation, as far as the locals were concerned. The shops and cafes were open for business, the children went off to school, and the farmers worked the land, and milked their cows. This was the lull before the man made storm.

At the coast, the German Army sentries', protected from the persistent rain and wind by their heavy bunkers, peered out over the beaches into the heavy swell of La Manche. They knew that Normandy was a possible target, and that the invasion would come soon somewhere, but no one believed that tonight would be the night. It was too rough. The sea was too choppy. The high command, including Field Marshal Rommel himself, had reached the same conclusion. The military weather forecasters had assured them that the poor weather would last for a few more days at least, making an invasion attempt at this time extremely unlikely.

The Germans had been convinced for some time that the Allied invasion would come in the first half of 1944, but they had been unable to penetrate the security ring around Overlord. Therefore, they had had to maintain coastal defences from Norway to the Spanish border. For tonight though, due to the inclement conditions they could relax. While the troops relaxed their vigilance, many senior officers made the 100-mile journey to Rennes to take part in a war game scenario organised for 7th Army personnel. Further, and crucially, Rommel had also taken advantage of the situation.

Convinced that the invasion was still several weeks away, the 'Desert Fox' had left for Germany on the previous Sunday, to spend some time with his family, and to seek a personal audience with Hitler. He planned to persuade the fuhrer to give him control of the panzer divisions in the west - which he believed would decide the outcome of the coming battle. With him, he had taken a new pair of shoes as a surprise for his wife, for in two days, 6th June, it would be her birthday.

On the afternoon of the fifth, on the other side of the Channel, Operation Neptune, the naval part of the invasion was underway. By late afternoon British and American minesweepers had cleared and marked a 5-mile radius of water near the Isle of Wight, and this zone, soon to become known with good reason as 'Piccadilly Circus', was where the 59 convoys of the five invasion fleets began to form up.

Once the fleet was assembled in the correct order the journey to the far shore began. Despite the vast scale of the fleet the Germans remained ignorant of the approaching threat. Allied bombers had destroyed many German radar installations in the weeks leading up to D-Day, and at that moment they were above the French coast dropping 'window' - foil strips that caused confusing echoes on the screens at the few remaining sites. Additionally, the poor weather had discouraged the German E-boats from patrolling, and while they remained in their protected pens at Le Havre and Cherbourg, the gigantic fleet moved ominously and unmolested towards its objective.

By the early hours of 6th June the greatest armada the world has ever seen lay off the Norman coast, ready to unleash its full fury on the unsuspecting enemy. On every craft in the fleet the tannoys came to life.

"Well we were woken at about 3.30am. I say 'woken' but we weren't getting much sleep anyway! A lot of the lads had just been lying around, chatting and playing cards, checking their equipment, things like that. The call came to 'Stand To' and to get to our posts, and after a bit Eisenhower's speech came over the tannoy."

Few men have ever been under the strain that the Supreme Commander was experiencing at this time, and the decision to launch the invasion played heavily on his mind. He spent the day before the landings visiting British troops, and also members of the American 101st Airborne Division at Greenham Common, in the hope that it would re-assure them and give them confidence. Most of the troops however, said later it felt like it was they that were reassuring him.

Out in the blackness of the Channel, as the fleet rose and fell on the heavy morning sea, the crowded decks fell silent as the strong, clear voice of General Eisenhower rang out. He had previously recorded an Order of the Day, and it was now being broadcast on the tannoys to inspire and focus the men for the task ahead.

'Soldiers, Sailors and Airmen of the Allied Expeditionary Force!

You are about to embark on the Great Crusade, toward which we have striven these many months. The eyes of liberty loving people everywhere march with you. In company with our brave Allies and brothers in arms on other Fronts, you will bring about the destruction of the German war machine, the elimination of Nazi tyranny over the oppressed people of Europe, and security for ourselves in a free world.

Your task will not be an easy one. Your enemy is well trained, well equipped and battle hardened. He will fight savagely.

But this is the year 1944! Much has happened since the Nazi triumphs of 1940-41. The United Nations have inflicted on the Germans great defeats, in open battle, man to man. Our air offensive has seriously reduced their strength in the air and their capacity to wage war on the ground. Our Home Fronts have given us an overwhelming superiority in weapons and munitions of war, and placed at our disposal great reserves of trained fighting men. The tide has turned! The free men of the world are marching together to Victory!

I have full confidence in your courage and devotion to duty and skill in battle. We will accept nothing less than full Victory! Good luck! And let us beseech the blessing of Almighty God upon this great and noble undertaking.'

General Dwight D. Eisenhower

Order of the day

6th June 1944

On the LCTs of the 86th Field Regiment, those who could manage it ate breakfast, and afterwards went about their business making final preparations for the task ahead. This was where the gruelling training began to pay dividends. Despite the fear and anxiety of some of the men, everyone knew their job and set about doing it. As they worked, the flames, explosions and tracer fire from the air bombardment lit up the night sky.

At around 05.30 the German batteries, by now finally aware of the fleet's presence, began to engage the armada. When the time came for the fleet to begin its own bombardment it was something that nobody there ever forgot.

"We had to pass through the fleet on the way in. I'll never forget that! 'Hellfire Pass' I called it! The noise from the battleships was incredible - you couldn't hear yourself think! They were firing big 14 and 16-inch shells. They sounded like railway cars going through the air! You could feel the draught of them going overhead, there was that many of them."

Many eyewitnesses to the naval bombardment have reiterated Ron's description of the event. The pulverising bombardment was intended to disable everything in the path of the advancing infantry – and ensure that any survivors were in no fit state to fight. Once again no chances were being taken. Despite the confidence of the Allied leaders they knew how capable and resolute the German soldier was and how well he could fight. Although having suffered hideous casualties on the Eastern Front over the previous two years, German strength in the West was still a force to be reckoned with.

No less than 38 Infantry Divisions guarded the French, Belgian, and Dutch coasts, with another ten in reserve. Additionally, a further ten Panzer (armoured) and mechanized divisions were stationed throughout France. It is true that the majority of the infantry troops stationed in the West were not of the calibre of their comrades on the Russian Front, but each one was at least capable of manning a machine-gun or a rifle from an entrenched defensive position.

These so-called 'inferior' troops also had the 'Atlantic Wall' to shield them, which despite being incomplete at the time of the invasion still represented a fearful obstacle to the assaulting forces.

Rommel had been horrified by its condition when inspecting it for the first time in 1943, and had immediately set about increasing its effectiveness. Within eight months his legendary drive and energy led to millions of tons of concrete being poured into hundreds of casemates and bunkers around likely landing sites, including the Mont Fleury and Longues batteries above Gold Beach.

On King sector, where the 86th was due to land, the sands were mined and zeroed for mortar, rifle, machine-gun, and artillery fire. Many houses behind the beach had been pulled down to improve fields of fire, or turned into fortresses. Also, Rommel had ordered the construction of a variety of deadly obstacles, many of which he had designed himself. Mined stakes and poles, 6-feet high steel rails welded together to form crosses which would stove in the bottoms of the landing craft, and other 'inventions' lay in wait for the attackers as they emerged from the surf. These obstacles were underwater at high tide, so their presence would force the Allies to land at low or half tide, leaving them with more of the fire-swept beach to negotiate.

Rommel, knowing full well that Allied air supremacy would prevent him from using his inland based panzer divisions to counter-attack, wanted to keep them as close to the coast as possible. He knew that if he could not defeat the invasion at the waters edge, it would be very difficult to dislodge the Allies once they were ashore.

His immediate superior, Field Marshal von Runstedt did not agree however, and preferred to keep the armour inland so that it could move quickly to wherever the main thrust of the invasion came. To complicate matters Hitler decreed that the armour could only be moved with his personal authority, a decision that would have grave consequences for him on D-Day. On board their LCTs on the morning of the sixth, the men of the 86th became aware of an awesome sight.

"As it got a bit lighter we began to see the size of the fleet around us. As far as you could see on either side,

80

and behind and in front, there were ships of every kind;
battleships, cruisers, LSIs, LCTs, infantry craft, all
sorts. You can't forget a sight like that. It made you feel
a part of something special.

We began our run-in shoot at about 06.45, 35 minutes
before the Green Howards were due to land, so we
were firing straight over their heads. We started firing
from about seven miles out, which is pretty much the
maximum range for the Sexton.

We were keeping up a steady rate of fire, about three
to four rounds per minute. Added to the racket from
the rest of the fleet the noise was deafening, and even
though we were practically standing next to each other
we had to shout to make ourselves heard."

The naval crews of the six LCTs carrying the regiment to the
shore had their work cut out keeping the 110-feet long craft on
a true course. The LCT was a notoriously difficult craft to steer,
and now in the choppy waters of this June morning, all skill and
knowledge was being tested to the limit to ensure that the course
remained true and that the regiment's guns were firing in the
right direction.

"It was about this time, around seven o'clock, that we
started seeing people thrashing about in the water.
They were survivors from the 'swimming' tanks
[Duplex Drive tanks fitted with a waterproof skirt].
Some of them had sunk before they'd reached the
shore! Blokes were struggling and screaming trying to

81

get out of them before they sank, but couldn't and got pulled down with them.

As we got closer and closer to the beach we could see the houses on the sea front on fire. Amid all the smoke and the din my mind wandered to thoughts of home.

My brother would be getting up for work, my mam would be getting my sister ready for school and would have just seen my dad off to work. That's the sort of thing that was going through my mind as we went in, and all I could think of was 'how the bloody hell did I end up here!'"

Despite Ron's reservations the operation was progressing remarkably well, with the volume and accuracy of the fire very consistent, a testament to the rigorous training the regiment had undergone. About ten minutes before the assault battalions landed, the guns of 86th Field Regiment switched to a new target.

"At about 1000 yards from shore we changed target. There was a fortified lighthouse on a hill above the beach and we went after that. We poured shells on to that place. By the time we landed we'd fired about 150 rounds per gun."

Once the first wave of infantry had landed on Gold Beach, about 15 minutes late at 07.45, 341, 342 and 462 batteries aboard the LCTs broke off their engagement with the lighthouse so that the crafts could turn about and leave the beach area clear for the next waves of the ground assault forces.

On the beach the Green Howards had made good ground. Having landed to the west of La Riviere, they fought their way up the beach and succeeded in destroying four pill-boxes and the strongpoint at nearby Hable-de-Heurtot, with the help of some AVREs - tanks fitted with a huge mortar designed to put concrete defences out of action. The decision to use specialised armour on the British beaches proved very wise indeed. The 'funnies', as they were affectionately known, were capable of performing a variety of tasks. Some were fitted with extended arms with thick chains attached, which rotated to clear a path through a minefield; some carried bridging equipment, a flamethrower, or coconut matting to negotiate soft ground. It was this ingenuity and improvisation that helped to give the attackers the upper hand.

While the Green Howards were engaging the German defences, the 86th was 'marking time' off shore, but soon received the order to make their final approach.

> "We came in the second time at about 08.30. By now the engineers had marked some lanes through the obstacles that they had made safe, but there was a lot of congestion because quite a few landing craft had been hit and had swung sideways in the water. We had a bit of a close shave, scraping down the side of another landing craft but apart from that our landing was good."

Further to the west, where 231st brigade was attacking in front of Le Hamel, the obstacles were causing major problems. No less than twenty LCTs were sunk or damaged in that sector; due to German snipers concentrating their fire on the underwater demolition teams that were trying desperately to disable the mines attached to the obstacles, and to clear paths for the approaching vessels.

At La Riviere the snipers had not been as effective and some lanes were already open by the time the LCTs of the 86th arrived.

"Our ramp went down in about a yard of water; whoever the captain of that LCT was, he did a good job that day. As we were preparing to disembark I had a good view down the beach both sides, and it looked a hell of a mess. There were wrecked landing craft and tanks ablaze, smoke, noise from machine-guns and artillery, houses on fire, it was terrible, it looked a real shambles.

We were the first artillery onto the beach, A, C, and E Troops. As we were just about to drive off down the ramp of the LCT, machine-gun fire hit a young sailor on board, although I didn't see what happened to him after that.

One thing about that day that will stay with me forever was when I saw a heavily loaded lad in front of our tank jump off the ramp into the water. He even had a folded bicycle strapped to his back. He jumped in and just vanished. He never surfaced. He must have fallen into an underwater shell hole and with all that gear on he never had a chance.

We had coconut matting, reinforced with iron bars, the 'roly-poly' we called it, laid out to give us some grip on the wet sand, and I remember being anxious because I could see big spouts of water landing around us. We didn't know if it was the Germans shelling us or if it was our own rounds falling short! Whatever it was it was too close for comfort!

We drove off to the waters edge and as soon as we were ready we started firing. Our FOOs [forward observation officers] had landed much earlier, and they were radioing targets to us. The noise was terrible, it was like being in a gale where you can't hear the person next to you, but what made it worse was we had to wear these little yellow earplugs to save our eardrums from the noise of our gun. It didn't help much though 'cos my hearing was never the same again anyway.

We came in just in front of a pillbox - it was disguised, but you could tell what it was. We had these 'porpoises', big metal cases full of ammunition tied onto the back of the Sexton, and one of jobs at the water's edge was to replenish the ammo' lockers 'cos we'd done a hell of a lot of firing on the way in.

That was the bit I really didn't like! We were running back and forth to the ammunition carrier nearby, carrying shells back to our tank, and cramming them

85

into every place we could find. After a bit we were so full we were a bit scared of getting an enemy round! It wasn't a very healthy place at the time, that's for sure! I'd promised my mam I'd come home, but on that beach that morning, I didn't think I'd be able to keep that promise.

There were bullets 'zinging' around, landing craft being tipped over or blown sky high by the mines on the obstacles, bodies and equipment floating in the water. Boys who'd been hit were struggling to pull themselves ashore out of the oncoming tide, but some of them couldn't move and just drowned where they were or were hit again.

This was going on all around you but you couldn't do anything about it; you just had to get on with your job. It was a shock to the system because this was our first action and it was a hell of a way to start, but it's your mates that keep you going; you'd be surprised.

You don't want to show fear in front of them, or let them down. I don't care who they are - private, captain, whatever - EVERYBODY on that beach was scared. I mean, I come from Birkenhead, a bloody rough bunch of buggers, but it would have frightened that lot as well! You take it, one minute there's a tank next to you with a bloke standing in the hatch, and the next minute he's got no head left, just blown off. It makes you think, that does.

It's very difficult to explain what it was like. You see photos of D-Day but you can't imagine the noise, or the smells of the fires and the cordite, or the screams of the wounded. They're the things that bring it back to me."

As the 86th was deploying and beginning to engage targets around the beach the reserve infantry battalion, the 7th Green Howards, was also coming ashore.

"Do you know, the thing that bothered me the most was the amount of time we were stationary on that beach, just parked there firing, only moving to keep ahead of the tide. We'd landed about half-an-hour too soon so we were there for longer than expected.

It scared me so much because during the crossing there had been an announcement on the tannoy that life expectancy on the beach would be about 30 minutes. They had the cheek to tell us that! I think they wanted to encourage us to keep going forward and to keep fighting until we got off the beach, but it didn't do much for your nerves!

Scampering back and forth to the ammo' lorry was horrible with all of that going on. Every time I got out of the tank I couldn't wait to get back in again! We'd been led to believe that there would be shell holes all over the beach, which would provide us with some cover, but for one reason or another the dropped bombs had missed and the beach was unmarked.

The RAF had Typhoons and Spitfires patrolling, laying

smokescreens, and strafing the Germans but we only saw two German planes the whole time that we were on the beach. Another one came along a bit later but he soon hightailed it as well.

There was one RAF regiment that must have had the worst job of all on D-Day. These blokes had to walk up and down the beach carrying a smaller version of a barrage balloon. It was a long piece of wire with a balloon filled with gas tied to the top, and it was to stop the enemy planes from strafing the infantry and tanks. I couldn't believe it when I saw that.

There was all sorts of equipment scattered on the beach by now because the second lot of infantry were wading ashore and when they were getting hit, packs of this and that were being washed in. We got quite a few 'compo' packs off the beach that way, 'cos we were there for quite a bit. We even managed to have a quick brew while we were waiting to get off, despite what was going on around us."

The fight for La Riviere was progressing well. The 6th and 7th Green Howards had silenced most of the pillboxes and bunkers in the area and were now looking to get the exit roads open so that the armour could breakout into the villages behind the beach.

By 10 o' clock the German resistance at King Green had been all but neutralised and a couple of the exits had been opened. At the same time B, D, and F Troops were disembarking from their

LCTs and getting ready for the drive inland.

"I can remember seeing D Troop land because my mate John shouted over to me. I didn't know what he was saying though because of all the bloody racket going on!

We were waiting in the traffic jam to get off the beach when I saw my first German soldiers. I can remember planes coming over and our infantry marching these POWs down onto the beach. From the look of them they weren't in very good shape at all. They looked dazed and scared. One of them had a hidden pistol on him and he shot himself right there in front of us.

Soon enough we were on our way off the beach. I can't remember to this day if we went up 'Lavatory Pan Alley', or up the exit road at Ver-Sur-Mer, where the Sexton memorial is now. As we were going up the road off the beach there were women and children throwing flowers and cheering us, even though a lot of the houses were on fire.

Mind you, there were some who weren't very pleased to see us at all. Some of them had German lovers, and children by them. They knew that our turning up would mean the end of that arrangement. You've got to remember that the Germans had been there for over four years."

It was 10.30 a.m. and 69th Brigade had completed the first stage of its objectives. The infantry and armour, aided greatly by the close fire-support from the 25-pdrs of the 86th, had stormed the beach defences and were ready to continue the advance inland. However, things were not going as smoothly elsewhere. At Le Hamel the 231st brigade were still involved in a furious fight in front of the massive strongpoint on that beach, and it would be mid-afternoon before the beach was deemed safe.

The Americans were also experiencing a day of mixed fortunes. At 'Utah' the furthest west of the landing sites, the troops had landed one and a half miles from their planned objective, but had quickly achieved their objectives anyway, and linked up with the airborne troops inland. 'Omaha', however, was where the Germans almost succeeded in stopping the attack. Assaulting an almost perfect 'killing ground' with very little armoured support, and facing a highly efficient and tough division of defenders, the U.S. 1st and 29th divisions suffered approximately 3,000 casualties, and by the end of the day still only held a tenuous foothold.

To the east of 'Gold', the Canadians at 'Juno' and the British 3rd Division at 'Sword' were well on their way to consolidating the beachhead despite some heavy casualties in the initial assault, and would soon meet the 6th British Airborne Division at Pegasus Bridge. Although the signs were good, the Allied commanders were not so foolish as to think that the job was over. They knew that although the Germans had been caught out, they would soon launch counter-attacks against the fragile beachhead, so it was vital that the momentum of the assault be maintained.

Rommel, racing back from Germany to conduct the German

defence, had contacted Hitler's HQ immediately, asking for the release of the panzer divisions. There followed one of the great ironies of the war; General Jodl, Hitler's Chief of Staff, informed Rommel that no decision on the armoured units could be taken at that moment because… the fuhrer was sleeping, and he had decreed that only he could signal their release. From the German perspective vital hours were lost which allowed the allies to consolidate their gains without the presence of enemy armour to worry them. Only 21st Panzer Division stationed around Caen, the Norman capital, was available but it would take some time to form up and move out.

The theme of the battle was now changing. The next phase would see the Allies attempt to keep the Germans on the back foot, while enough supplies and reinforcements were brought ashore for future operations. As soon as Gold and the other beaches had been cleared of enemy troops the supply battle began. Within hours the necessary reinforcements, vehicles, equipment, food and medicine had begun to come ashore.

Now that the beach had been negotiated and all of the 86th's batteries were back together, they headed, with their respective infantry battalions, for the nearby Mont Fleury battery, a German stronghold positioned on the hill above La Riviere.

"We dumped the 'porpoises' on the side of the road and set off for Mont Fleury, but we got held up almost straight away by snipers. At La Riviere there was a little café on the corner and there was sniper fire coming from around there, so one of our officers

wanted volunteers to go and sort it out. As you can imagine, he got loads of offers!! Anyway, they started to pick 'volunteers' when no one had stepped forward, unmarried men first.

Well I got picked; so off up the road a few of us went, hearts pounding. I think there were some Scotch lads in front of us and they had the Bren gun. They sprayed it into the trees by the café and the sniper fell to the floor dead. It was a bloody French woman! That happened a few times. Like I said, some of them weren't happy to see us at all."

The key to the advance now, was speed. The infantry were pushing inland to Crepon and to the east and west, in an attempt to enlarge the beachhead so reinforcements could land more quickly, and also to link up with units coming from the other beaches. The large town of Bayeux, famous for its tapestry, was the 50th Division's main target for the day, and 3-4 miles to the east of it, on either side of the N13, the main Caen-Bayeux road, sat the tiny village of St.Leger.

If 69 Brigade, and its supporting units (including the 86th) could capture the village quickly it would slow the Germans ability to transfer armour and troops from Caen to the Cherbourg peninsula, where the Americans would soon attempt to capture the deepwater port there.

"It was basically a mad dash. We pushed onto Mont Fleury and not long after to a position near Ver-sur-Mer so that we could begin firing in support of the

Green Howards as they advanced on Crepon and
Creully. There was an important bridge there and we
were pouring shells onto the Germans in that area."

As the batteries of the 86th launched shell after shell into the enemy positions, the Green Howards were fighting their way forward against increasingly stiff opposition from the battle-hardened 352nd Division. Luckily, Kampfgruppe Meyer, a crack formation stationed at Bayeux, had been receiving all kinds of confusing reports and had spent the whole morning marching about the Normandy countryside on a variety of false alarms. This enabled the British to capture Creully and its vital bridge, but just as the road to Bayeux looked open, the Germans appeared to check the advance, with the village of St. Leger still 1000 yards beyond.

The 86th was still positioned around Ver-sur-Mer by nightfall, and like everyone else on the battlefield, the men of C Troop were completely exhausted.

"You think; we were up at 3.30 a.m. that day and apart
from the odd brew, we didn't have anything proper to
eat or drink until after midnight."

As the advance slowed, orders were passed down from 69 Brigade HQ to hold positions for the night.

"We were ready for a rest by that point and I remember
looking for a place to sleep. Me and my mate Peter
reckoned that the safest place to be was on the other
side of a wall next to where our tank was parked. I
thought that if anything was going to hit me it would

have to come through the tank and then through the wall first!

It was pitch black; we couldn't see a thing, so when we climbed over the wall we thought we'd landed in a slit trench. Anyway, I didn't mind, we had a smoke and some compo'rations and I don't know where he got it, but Peter had found a bottle of wine, so we shared that as well.

The following morning when we woke up we saw that we'd been sleeping in a grave! When we looked over to the corner by the wall there were three dead Germans lying there!"

Lying in the darkness, amid the flashes of the naval guns, twenty-year-old Ron reflected on the events of a day he would never forget.

"It was only when you stopped to think that it got to you. I thought to myself, 'If I can get through this, I'll stick the rest.' It was terrible, horrific; there were a few blokes who packed it in after that, they did everything they could not to go any further.

Seeing lads that you didn't even know lying dead or dying on the beach; it stays with you. You wonder why you hadn't been hit. |It was different later in the campaign because the more you see, the tougher you get. The only thing that happened to us during the day was someone attached a 'sticky' bomb to the side of the tank, but we were OK because they hadn't put it onto the track.

There was a lot that weren't so lucky though...poor buggers...they're the ones you feel sorry for."

The 6th June had indeed been all of the things that Ron described. However, it had also been a stunning success from the commanders' perspective, as all five beachheads had been captured and were in the process of being consolidated and reinforced.

On Gold Beach 25,000 troops had come ashore during the day for the loss of 413 killed, wounded, or missing. Admittedly, Bayeux had not been captured, nor had the road between it and Caen, but the signs were good. Tomorrow, 7th June, the infantry would renew their advance and the 86th would be going with them, but for Ron and everyone else who took part, 6th June was 'the longest day'.

"If anyone ever says they went through Hell on D-Day, they're telling the truth; they CAN say, 'I have been there.'"

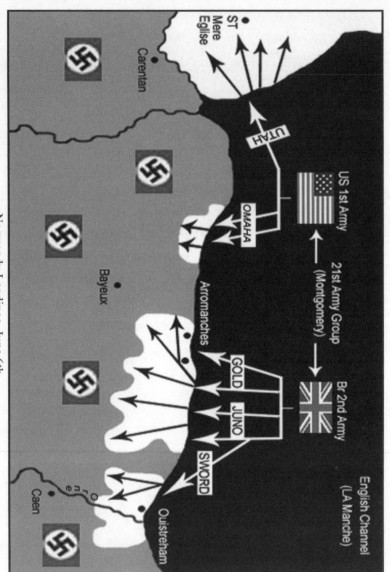

Normandy Landings, June 6th

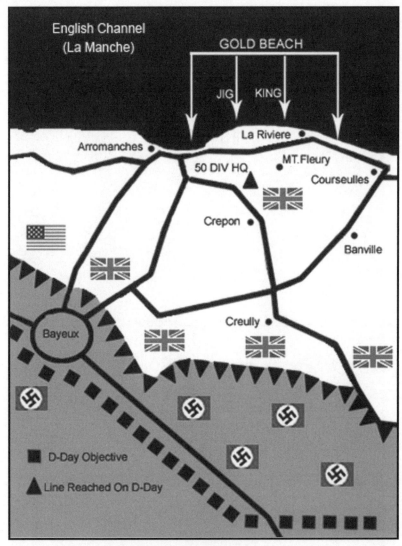

Advancement of 50th Division on D-Day

Chapter Six

The Struggle Inland

7th June – 21st August 1944

As dawn crept over the Norman countryside on 7th June, press and radio around the world were already reporting the events of the previous day. In Britain, the daily newspapers proclaimed in bold type, 'INVASION!' or something akin to it; and over their breakfast men and women throughout the land read in awe of the exploits and achievements of the previous day. People everywhere were overjoyed at the news, and it soon became the only topic of conversation..

Ron, lying in a damp grave in a field in Normandy, didn't share their enthusiasm.

> *"I've got to admit, after D-Day I was glad to see the seventh, but now that I knew what was ahead of me, I can't say I was looking forward to it. I have to say that even though we'd been trained to the highest level, if we'd have known what we were letting ourselves in for, they'd have had a job to get us on the boat!"*

Despite the unquestioned success of the previous day the men of the regiment knew that it was just the beginning, and that there was a lot of hard fighting ahead of them. Early that morning, after they'd eaten some compo' rations and shaken the cold and stiffness from their tired bodies, it was back to work. The immediate objective remained the village of Crepon, about three miles to the south, where the infantry had met stiff resistance as they battled to reach the Caen-Bayeux road.

As the morning wore on the last remaining resistance at Crepon succumbed to the British attack and it was soon time for the 86th to get back on the road and head for their next gun position - a wooded area near the village of St. Gabriel, on the outskirts of Creully; where the regiment set about shelling enemy positions around the important cross roads in the village of Jerusalem.

"Jerusalem must have looked like a pepper-pot after we'd finished with it. It was only a small village but they fought like fanatics to hold on to it. We pounded the place with shells; and on top of that lot, the bombers flattened it from the air."

On 7th June the 50th Division had reaped the rewards of its excellent performance of the previous day. Bayeux, the most prized of the D-Day objectives for those landing on Gold Beach, was 'captured' virtually intact, the term being used loosely as its defenders had hastily evacuated the ancient town on D-Day. However, away to the east, Caen, the capital was still very much in German hands and heavily protected - both sets of commanders appreciating the importance of the city.

Situated ten miles from the coast at the mouth of the river Orne, Caen's port, road, and rail network made it the key to the Allied advance in the east. The rolling plains around the town were ideal for tanks and offered a quick route to Paris, about 100 miles away on the Seine. Like Bayeux, it had been a D-Day objective, but in hindsight this had been a very ambitious goal, as nearly all of the German armour available in the east was positioned in a protective ring around the city. The British 3rd Division coming from Sword Beach on the left flank, and the Canadian 3rd Division, had been aiming to capture Carpiquet, the airfield just west of the city, but despite valiant efforts the 21st and 12th SS Panzer Divisions had stopped them in their tracks.

The Allied position was still far from secure at this point but thanks to the spectacular success of Operation Fortitude (a complex deception plan that suggested that the main assault was still to come in the Pas-de-Calais region), the full weight of the German Army had not yet been hurled at the invasion forces.

General Montgomery, in overall command of the Allied forces, knew full well that time was of the essence when he came ashore at Gold on 8th June to establish his field headquarters. He believed it was vital the momentum of the assault be maintained, but after studying the reports of the situation around Caen, he announced that he intended to alter some aspects of the next phase of the assault.

He realised that a frontal assault on the city would be both costly and time consuming, so to avoid this he decided to skirt around the town from both sides, cut it off, and then continue the attack south, towards the town of Falaise, the gateway to Paris. For the proposed attack he would use the 51st (Highland) Division on the left flank, and the 7th Armoured Division, the famous 'Desert Rats' who had gained fame in the North African campaign, on the right. 7th Armoured, with the 86th Field Regiment now transferred to it for the attack, would advance along the general line of the village of Tilly-sur-Seulles, and onto Villers-Bocage, an important road junction that, if it could be captured, would open the way to Falaise from the west.

The attack began on 10th June and was met by fierce resistance at every turn, resulting in appalling casualties on both sides. The terrain was as much of a barrier as the Germans were, as this part of Normandy, the bocage, was a formidable obstacle in its own right. The sunken roads, orchards, thick stonewalls, and high, dense hedgerows were a defenders' dream, and the Germans used every aspect of the land to their advantage. A well-sighted 88mm, MG42, or camouflaged sniper could wreak havoc on a much larger force in this contained environment, but options were limited from an Allied perspective.

As Tilly was proving almost as difficult to capture as Caen, an attempt was made to overrun Villers Bocage from another village, Caumont, about five miles to the west, where a possible gap in the German line had been spotted. However, this attack, carried out on 13th June ended in complete disaster for the British when their tanks entered Villers Bocage and encountered a group of Tiger tanks commanded by Michael Wittman, Germany's leading tank ace. By the end of the battle the British had lost over fifty tanks and armoured vehicles, and the gap in the German line had been closed.

Despite the exhaustion of both sides, the battle to capture Tilly and the neighbouring village of Lingevres continued. The strategic importance of the area was evident from the savage nature of the fighting. For the 86th the following week was an exhausting one. 342 Battery fired thousands of rounds as they worked overtime supporting the relentless infantry assaults on those villages. On the 14th, troops of the Durham Light Infantry, with 342 Battery in direct support, finally dislodged the last remaining resistance from Lingevres, and on the 20th Tilly was captured. Men who fought at the battle of Tilly have described it as being as fierce as any combat that they experienced during the war. By the time the British at last gained full possession of it on June 20th, Tilly had changed hands 23 times.

"It was a terrible battle, Tilly. By the time we'd captured it the whole area was smashed, it was just rubble, [The remaining parts of the village had to be demolished after the battle.] but our efforts weren't in vain. Monty sent every man in 50th Div' a gift of five cigarettes each after that battle. He was very good to us, was Monty; twice in the whole campaign he did that!"

On the day before Tilly fell, the 86th was transferred to support the 50th Division's attack on Hottot, the next village on the way to Villers Bocage, and during this battle the commander of 342 Battery, Major Swann, was killed. His men keenly felt his loss, as he had always led the battery by example, and had played a major role in the capture of Lingeveres, for which he had been awarded the Military Cross. During the next few days, with the battle for Hottot still raging, Captain Robert Kiln was promoted to the rank of major and posted to command of 342 Battery. The following two weeks were a little less frantic, although contact with the enemy was maintained, and the pressure on Hottot kept up.

The reason for the relative lull in the British operations was due to supply problems. On 19th June a great storm had hit Normandy, the like of which had not been seen in the area for eighty years. For three days it lashed the coast, destroying everything in its path. The Mulberry Harbour at Omaha Beach was totally destroyed, but Mulberry B at Arromanches, although heavily damaged, resumed operations after repairs. The situation was critical; 140,000 tons of supplies and 800 ships were lost or beached. The effects on the men in the field were both immediate and serious. It now became all the more important that the deepwater port at Cherbourg be captured.

The 86th was immediately cut back to thirty rounds of ammunition per gun daily, although this did not include 'major operations'. This was just as well because Operation Epsom, Monty's long delayed plan to outflank Caen from the west, was scheduled to start as soon as possible. To conduct Epsom 60,000 men, 600 tanks, and 700 field guns had been assembled. The Sextons of the 86th were now stationed close to the village of Chouain, near Tilly, and at 04.15 on the morning of the 26th, the opening barrage began.

Epsom was designed to outflank Caen, a manoeuvre that would threaten the encirclement of the Germans defending the city. This would draw German armour away from the American sector in the west, which would facilitate a breakthrough by the U.S. forces there, in the St. Lo area. As usual, Epsom began with a bang, but within four days the Allies suffered 4,000 casualties without making any significant gains. The Germans had also suffered heavy losses, and although no breakthrough was achieved, the Allied attacks were having an effect. The following weeks saw 86th Field Regiment supporting various infantry units in attacks on Hottot and the surrounding villages. Every day was dangerous, tiring work and the men badly needed a break, but at the moment there seemed no chance of a rest.

"The battles around Caen went on for about six weeks and that's when you start getting edgy. When you're fighting for weeks and weeks on end and hardly moving, it worries you. The boredom, the waiting, we weren't getting anywhere, even though we were belting Hell out of 'Jerry' and he was belting Hell out of us. Rumours were going around that the invasion had ground to a halt.

The monotony starts eating away at your nerves. Every day seems the same as the last one. We'd be supporting all sorts of infantry attacks. One day we'd move up a couple of miles to help one group out, but the next day we might move back to our original positions for another unit.

At that point we spent about eighty per cent of the time in and around the cornfields on the outskirts of the city. We were never far from the tank; we always slept in a trench nearby. We felt very exposed, and cover was always a concern, 'cos the land there is so flat. The Germans used to dig their Tigers and Panthers in, so that only their turret was above ground level. In the long grass the infantry only found out where they were when it was too late.

We used to have to interrupt the fire-plan and keep moving around the fields so that Jerry couldn't get his range on us with his big guns, 'cos if he did get a line on you he wouldn't let you go. Every ten minutes or so

106

he'd give us a good burst just to let us know that he was still there!

We'd position the guns, and then as soon as possible we'd dig a slit trench nearby for cover while we were waiting for our fire-plan. The trouble was, we had to keep moving around to avoid being zeroed, so we'd end up digging two or three trenches a day. I remember a couple of lads from a regiment next to us being killed. They used to sleep underneath their tank for protection, but one night the tank's tracks sunk ever so slowly, and crushed the pair of them.

At night, the Germans used to use a lot of 'Molotov Baskets'; they were incendiaries and very effective. When they went off it was like daylight, you could read a newspaper. Then, when they got a fix on our positions, their bombers would come in.

Another thing springs to mind from the time around Caen. At night, the Germans had a van or lorry driving up and down their front line with a big tannoy system on it. We couldn't see it obviously, but we'd hear this woman's voice saying things like, 'Hello Tommy, How are you? Are you enjoying yourselves, because the Yanks are! They're having a nice time back home with your wives and sweethearts!'

It would go on all night, blaring out like that. If anything it raised morale! It used to give us a bloody good laugh."

On 7th July, 450 Allied bombers dropped 2,500 tons of bombs onto the centre of Caen, causing untold casualties and damage but enabling British and Canadian infantry to begin the liberation of the city. The Southern suburbs however, remained in German hands. The same day the 86th moved to new gun positions near the village of La Belle Epine, to support another attack on Hottot. Once again they were driving through shattered villages bearing the scars of war. Knocked out tanks, smashed houses, and decomposing corpses of men and cattle, were a common sight. It was at these moments that Ron reflected on the realities of the war.

"When you're a gunner, it's not like being in the infantry. We were ramming the shells into the gun and firing all day sometimes, but you never stop to think where that shell's heading or the damage it's going to do. It's when you drive up through afterwards and see these places you've been fighting for; that's what makes you stop and think."

By the morning of 16th July, the regiment was in open positions at Fontenay les Pesnil, a few miles east of Tilly, in the wide expanses of the Norman cornfields. This was to be the preliminary attack of Operation Goodwood, Monty's last big hope of breaking through around Caen. Over the next four days the air forces dropped thousands of tons of bombs, and the artillery unleashed a devastating bombardment, with 341 Battery alone firing nearly 3,000 rounds on the opening day. In the German positions 60-ton Tiger tanks were flipped upside down by the ferocity of the bombardment, but when the infantry attacked, the surviving Germans emerged to hold the Allies back and continued to bar the way to Falaise.

"I remember when we were trying to break through to Villers-Bocage, we were called to give some fire support to some infantry who were attacking a chateau. After we'd moved up and shelled it, the Germans that had survived, started to stumble out. Their C.O. looked like he'd come straight from the parade ground! He was immaculate! We sent them all back as prisoners."

On the 19th rumours began to spread among the men of the regiment that they were moving out of the line. They had often heard this but nothing had ever come of it, so nobody got too excited. The following day however, to their utter relief, the rumour became reality and the move to St. Andre, a village five miles to the south of Bayeux, got under way. The regiment had been in constant action since D-Day; 44 consecutive days, and was in real need of a rest.

"We were in a terrible state! When we first got drawn out of the line, we were taken to a place near Bayeux in 3-tonners. There was a big chateau there with a tent attached to the archway. You had to go into the tent, strip off and get de-loused with this powder called DDT. After that we had our first shower since D-Day! It was paradise! It was Heaven! Up until then we'd had to make do with streams and rivers to keep ourselves clean, which wasn't ideal, but we'd managed.

When the weather was good we used to dry our clothes on the engine of the tank. After the shower we were given new uniforms. You don't know what that was like!"

Although they were out of the line for 'rest', the men were still expected to undertake chores and duties.

"For the first few days we couldn't really relax because there was a lot of stuff to do. Behind the front line Army life kicked back in and we had the usual things like inspections and maintenance. We didn't mind though because we had good food, cinema shows (we saw Bing Crosby in 'Going my way?), games, and lots of nice girls to keep us company! We also went into Bayeux to see the Tapestry.

We really needed that break. When you're in the line you have to carry on, physically and mentally, but you can't go on forever; you have to have a rest at some point. The trouble was, within a couple of weeks of going back into the line, we were back in the same state."

Just being out of the line, where the ever-present danger of a sniper's bullet or an enemy shell shredded the nerves and sapped the energy of the men, was sufficient to rejuvenate their spirits. The physical and mental strain of combat had taken its toll, but really it was only when the men were removed from the combat zone that thoughts of injury or death came to the fore.

On 28th July the regiment moved back into the line. The new gun positions were near La Belle Epine, but by the time the guns were in action, rumours of a big move were sweeping through

110

the ranks. Since D-Day, the American forces west of Gold, had been fighting their way up the Cherbourg peninsula, and on 27th June had succeeded in capturing the town and its vital port, which the German defenders had crippled before the G.I.s' arrival. The Americans now turned south again, and on 25th July, while Ron and the men of the 86th were enjoying their well-earned rest, the breakout from the US sector began.

Operation Cobra involved the U.S. forces punching a hole through the German defences to the west of St. Lo, a pivotal town below the Cherbourg Peninsula, and it was now that the British pressure in the east began to tell. With the German armour being used to repel the British around Caen, the Americans attacked, and broke through the thin crust as planned. The American Third Army, under General George Patton, was now let off the leash and began advancing west into Brittany, and up behind the German defences around Caen, which were also trying to deal with 'Bluecoat', another major British attack from the north.

The German commanders quickly spotted the danger to their forces. With the British and Canadians pressing them from the north, and the Americans sweeping up behind them from the south and west, the Germans would be caught in the middle, around Falaise. If this encirclement were to happen it might mean the end for the entire Fifth and Seventh Armies. The only chance was to begin an immediate withdrawal east, where the natural barrier of the River Seine, and reinforcements from the Pas de Calais area might stem the Allied advance.

The race began. In early August the Germans began heading east through a gap between the towns of Falaise in the north, and Argentan in the south, a corridor about 25 miles wide. Over 100,000 soldiers, armoured cars, half-tracks, tanks, horse-drawn wagons and gun-carriages moved bumper to bumper along the minor roads and lanes of the escape route - easy pickings for the Allied artillery and fighter-bombers.

"It was good to be actually moving again. We'd been static for so long. We began advancing quite quickly and sometimes we'd catch some Germans who hadn't managed to get away in time. We caught a German paymaster near Villers-Bocage. One of the lads went up to him and went to take his wallet, but the German asked in broken English if he could keep the photos of his mother and his family. We checked inside the case he was carrying and it was stuffed full of French francs! It must have been the pay for his whole company! We shared it out between us all. We were flush for a good while after that.

If we were billeted in or around a village, and if we weren't on duty, we could go and have a drink and something to eat in a café if it hadn't been evacuated or destroyed. I remember we stopped at one little village and there was a group of people having their photograph taken outside a café. It was a wedding, and they grabbed me and Peter and a couple of other lads to pose with them. After that they invited us in to the café for a drink, and we remembered that we still had all of this money from the German on us.

We gave all the kids twenty Francs each, which was a lot, and we gave the bride a 1,000 franc note, which would have probably bought a house back then. She was so excited that she ran up the stairs and I tell you, we didn't know who was going to have the first night, the groom or us!! Money meant very little to us in that environment.

That same night, we caught ten or twelve Germans in the village, and met up with some members of the local French Resistance. We didn't have any way to take the prisoners with us so we handed them over to the partisans, who said that they'd take them back to the beaches. They'd only got around the corner when we heard the rattle of sub-machine-guns and rifle fire! When we looked the Germans were lying dead in a heap in the road. A lot of that went on."

Over the next two weeks every road in the corridor became a scene of suffering and devastation as the Allies poured shell after shell, and bomb after bomb into the beleaguered, retreating columns. Valiant efforts were made by some SS units to hold the Allies back, so that the retreating forces would have more time to escape, but the outcome was inevitable.

"You had to see it, and SMELL it, to believe it. Since we'd come ashore in June the weather had been mostly very good; which you appreciate when you're sleeping outdoors every night, but it also meant that the smell

from the rotting bodies and cattle was overpowering sometimes.

On those roads to Falaise it got to the point that we didn't know what we were driving over. It wasn't as if you could avoid it, there were smashed tanks, guns, gear, and everywhere you looked dead and dying German soldiers and horses. It was horrible. If ever there was a killing ground that was it.

Eisenhower visited the area soon after and when he said that you could walk for hundreds of yards at a time across the dead bodies, he wasn't exaggerating. I'd seen plenty of corpses by that point and had become pretty much used to it, but there was one thing that always stuck in my mind during the breakout.

We were driving down a road on the way to Falaise and there was a knocked out, burning Panther tank in the ditch at the side of the road. As we passed it I saw one of the worst sites I ever saw. A German soldier must have been trying to get out of the turret after it had been hit but he hadn't made it. He'd been burnt to a crisp and had actually become welded to the steel of the tank. He looked like a little black doll. It was terrible, that.

A bit later on, near Argentan, we went into a café and in one of the back rooms there was a pile of dead French women lying all around. They were pregnant and they'd all been bayoneted, and we found out later

114

it was because they'd been German sympathisers and were carrying the children of the occupation troops.

We weren't just giving harassing fire during the breakout. A lot of the time we were up front in direct support of the infantry. If they were being held up in a town or village, we'd be called to shell the place or to blast a strongpoint.

The Germans were sometimes so close you could hear them. They had this thing called a Nebelwerfer, 'moaning minnies' the Yanks called them. It looked a bit like a field kitchen; it had big pipes on it that fired rockets and mortars. It made my blood curdle, that thing! We could sometimes hear the Germans putting the shells in and slamming the breech shut; we were that close."

On 17th August the 86th had arrived at the town of Flers, and been transferred to the 11th Armoured Division. The volume of Allied traffic engaged in the breakout was staggering. The Military Police, situated at every crossroads and junction along the route, performed miracles co-ordinating the access for the multitude of units descending upon them, but they did receive some help. At Flers, the civilian population gave their liberators a rapturous welcome and some members of the Free French were so overjoyed that they took to directing the traffic themselves!

Since the beginning of the offensive, the batteries had supported infantry attacks by units of the 50th and 43rd Divisions, and had operated from gun positions at Jurques, Les Moeux, Proussy, Briouze, and Ecouche. A cause of real satisfaction for the men was their contribution to the capture of Mont Pincon, a 400-metre ridge that was the dominating feature of the Norman landscape, on which they later established a new gun position.

From the crest of Mont Pincon the plight of the trapped German Armies was clearly visible. In every smashed and burning village in the 'pocket', evidence of unsuccessful German attempts to stem the Allied advance was plainly visible. As their situation became more desperate by the hour, their ability to offer any real organised resistance diminished. Indeed, towards the end of the assault on the 'Falaise pocket', it was getting difficult for the Allied gunners to put down accurate fire, because the Germans were retreating so quickly that the forward observers had trouble keeping in contact with them.

The final days of the Falaise campaign were a continuation of the slaughter of the previous week, as the noose slipped tighter and tighter around the neck of the beleaguered German forces. Although the Allies paused at a critical point, which allowed some of the enemy forces to escape, the passage was finally slammed shut on 21st August between Trun and Chambois, two villages a few miles to the east of Falaise and Argentan.

Amid the chaos, around 20,000 troops of the Seventh Army had managed to evade the Allied forces and make their way east. Despite this, the two German Armies had been practically annihilated, and the remnants of those once mighty formations that had escaped the carnage amounted to nothing more than a

116

disorganised rabble. Inside the 'pocket' the destruction was indescribable. Ten thousand dead, and over nine thousand pieces of artillery, tanks, guns, and cars littered the battlefield. Also, fifty thousand German troops were now being shepherded into prisoners-of-war cages.

The Battle of Normandy was over, and for the Germans it had ended disastrously. Within three months of the landings they had been comprehensively defeated in the field. To compound this, the Russian summer offensive had recently begun, and forced the German line on the Eastern Front back past its 1941 starting point, destroying twelve top-notch German divisions in the process.

Adolf Hitler's forces were reeling. The Allied commanders were sure that all that was needed now was the final knockout punch, but as we shall see, the German Army in the West would prove them wrong.

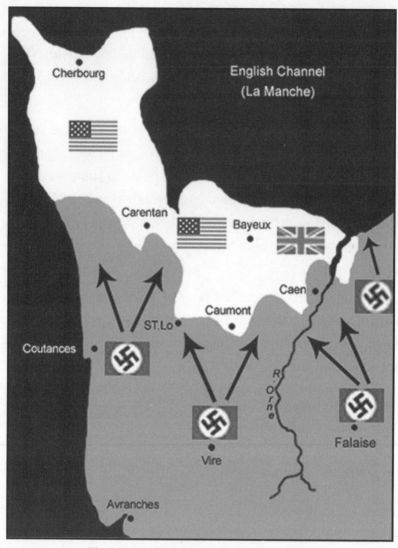

The Normandy Bridgehead, 29th June 1944

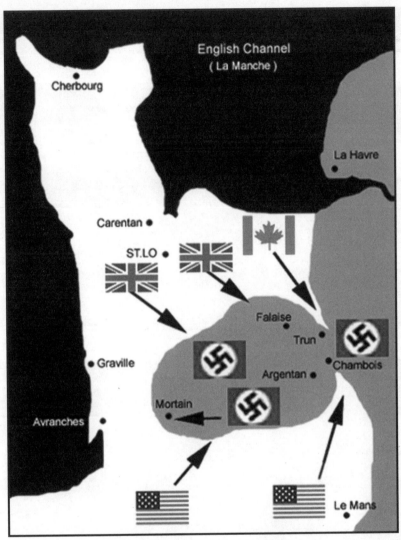

The Falaise Pocket, August 1944

Chapter Seven

The Pursuit

22nd August - 16th September 1944

At the planning stage, Operation Overlord had only been projected as far as the Allied armies reaching the River Seine. It had been considered too complex to attempt to lay down operational timetables after that point, due to the numerous variables involved in a campaign of this size. Throughout the hierarchy of the Allied command it had been generally agreed that it would be at the Seine that the Germans would attempt to regroup and form a new defensive line. This proved an accurate assessment.

It was also appreciated that the Allied supply system would be under greater strain than ever before. The vast majority of stocks were still coming in to the battle from the beachheads won on D-Day, and this obviously meant that the rapid advance would take the units further away from the ammunition dumps and supply areas on which they depended. Therefore it was critical that an adequate logistic structure be established for the next phase of the campaign.

For the Allied commanders, the supply situation had to be balanced against the military implications of a halt. Although the German forces that had escaped the Falaise pocket were in a poor state, they had managed to construct a pontoon bridge across the Seine by August 23rd, giving them a chance to throw up a semblance of organised defence on the eastern bank of the great river. This was exactly what the Allies didn't want to happen. Eisenhower wanted to keep the enemy off balance and drive him back across France and into Germany.

The Supreme Commander had adopted a 'broad front' policy.

He felt that if the Allies advanced in this way it would stretch the enemy everywhere, not allowing them to offer any real, determined resistance. Putting this plan into action he sent Bradley's forces, the American armies, east towards Luxembourg and Saar, the important German industrial region, while Twenty-First Army Group under Montgomery quickly received the order to cross the Seine and 'destroy all enemy forces in the Pas-de-Calais and Flanders, and to capture Antwerp.'

The British Second Army's role in this would be to cross the Seine, drive north, and with all speed secure the area Amiens-St.Pol-Arras. This advance would in theory have many advantages. It would eliminate the last sizable German forces in Western Europe, cut off or capture the ports of Bolougne, Dunkirk, and Calais, and overrun the V-weapon launching sites - Hitler's latest terror weapon. Further, it would gain vital airfields, and seize the port of Antwerp, a particularly prized goal, as it would greatly ease the impending Allied fuel crisis.

This was no easy task. It would be drive of about 200 miles through territory that the enemy had held for over four years, and before anyone went anywhere a secure bridgehead would have to be established over the Seine. This task was given to the 43rd Division and while they were carrying it out, the 11th Armoured Division, to which 86th Field Regiment was still attached, was withdrawn from action for five days of rest and maintenance. As always it was a much-appreciated break from front-line duty.

At dawn on 29th August the vehicles and men of the 11th Armoured Division finally arrived at their crossing in the town of Vernon, about fifty miles southwest of Paris. They had travelled ninety miles through the night along roads clogged with traffic. Soon after arrival, although exhausted by the journey the regiment rumbled over the recently constructed pontoon bridge that had been built next to the tangled wreckage of the original iron bridge; destroyed by Allied bombing earlier in the campaign.

Ahead lay the wide-open spaces of the French countryside, and this was how the armoured units had envisaged the war; fast moves and rapid gains. The tank crews and gunners that had been part of the grinding stalemate around Caen in the earlier part of the campaign were now in their element, and morale was extremely high.

"The amount of vehicles and troops crossing the river was unbelievable. With that many vehicles on the road the dust was terrible. Our throats were parched and we had to wear goggles, and tie handkerchiefs around our faces to keep the dust out; it helped, but during the hot weather it was still very uncomfortable.

Crossing France we tried to use the fields as much as we could because the traffic on the roads was bumper to bumper, and it cut down on the dust. Using the fields meant that it could still be a very bumpy ride. It was almost like being on a landing craft; the tank would go over a hedge or a ditch, and come down hard, like hitting a wave. The good thing about it though was that there were plenty of rails and bars to hold onto.

The Sexton performed exceptionally well during the drive north. I think we only had one breakdown during the whole journey, and that was when we lost a track. There were two fitters in the troop and they'd perform all the essential maintenance whenever it was needed. We'd leave that side of things to them and concentrate on making sure that the ammunition lockers were kept full, and that the gun, and the rest of our kit and equipment was in as good as working order as possible."

The pursuit of the Germans continued. Every so often the regiment would receive orders to fire on a nearby enemy resistance point, but in the main the only Germans the regiment saw at this point were the columns of prisoners marching back past the advancing Allied armour and into captivity.

The following days were a highpoint for the men of the regiment. Racing on to their objectives, they were treated as heroes at every village, and received gifts of fruit, wine, cider, and other contraband items that had been successfully concealed from the Germans during the occupation. The advance continued day and night. When darkness fell the Sextons would be reduced to a steady crawl along the packed roads with only the shaded convoy light of the vehicle in front offering any assistance to the bleary-eyed drivers.

"They pushed us hard. You slept and ate when you

could. At a stopping point you'd just grab some compo
and try to shut your eyes for a bit, if you weren't on
guard duty."

This relentless pursuit was not in vain. By the afternoon of 31st August the 11th Armoured Division had entered Amiens, a major city situated on the River Somme, amid joyous scenes. Further, prior to the division's arrival the Germans had been driven from several key bridges in the area before they'd had the opportunity to destroy them. This was drastic from their point of view. With the bridges in Allied hands the Germans would have no time to form a defensive line at this natural barrier and once again, as at the Seine, they would have to continue their retreat to the next place that would facilitate a co-ordinated, organised defence.

By the evening of 2nd September the regiment had crossed Vimy Ridge, immortalised by the Canadian attack there during the Great War, aided in the liberation of Lens, and were now in action on the northern outskirts of that town.

"I remember when we stopped somewhere near the
Belgian border a parcel arrived in the mail for me. I
opened it up and it was a birthday cake that my mam
had made for me and sent over. It had only taken five
months! It was in a round tin and as a treat she'd put
woodbine fags all around the edge for me.

By the time it got to me the cake was rock hard and the
tobacco had come out and got mixed in with the cake!
My mates and me hammered it and mixed it up with

milk and put it on a primus stove. It wasn't bad! I was
21 years old."

Lille was the next major town on route to Antwerp, but enemy resistance stiffened markedly as the convoy reached its suburbs. German troops, hidden in a wooded area near the road, and armed with a camouflaged 88mm gun, destroyed six or seven lorries containing ammunition. By chance the 86th was near the scene and Major Corke, commanding 341 Battery, immediately set off in a jeep to survey the situation. As the jeep passed a burning vehicle some of the ammunition within exploded with deadly force. Major Corke was killed instantly, and Gunner Brown, driving the jeep, was blown through the windscreen and severely wounded.

A little further ahead near Avelin, there was more trouble. A German six-gun field battery hidden near a chateau and its surrounding woods was now firing directly at the Allied vehicles as they moved up the road. Major Scammel of 462 Battery and Sergeant Burgess of D Troop quickly did a recce on foot, and shortly afterwards the latter took his Sexton across open ground and began shelling the chateau, all the time under heavy fire. After several rounds had entered the building a white flag appeared and the Germans surrendered. A mopping up operation ensued and after the surrounding woods had been cleared, the British took over one hundred prisoners of differing ranks.

The advance could now continue, but almost immediately some German tanks, hidden on the other side of the road, entered the fray and began firing on the advancing column. Orders quickly came for 342 Battery to lay a smokescreen so that vehicles, which could not get off the road, at least had some cover as they raced through the hotspot. For his actions in the earlier incident, Sergeant Burgess received the Military Medal. These incidents were a timely reminder that even during this exhilarating period, the war and what it entailed, was never far away.

Mid afternoon on the 3rd saw the regiment crossing the Franco-Belgian border to a rapturous welcome; village streets along the route were packed with the local populace, eager to offer gifts and thanks to their liberators amidst a carnival atmosphere. Further, more and more Germans were losing the race to stay out of the clutches of their pursuing enemy, and during the 'mopping up' the prisoner count was climbing rapidly.

"There was a hell of a lot of Germans giving themselves up. We'd given them a real pounding and a lot of them just wanted it over with. The people in these places loved us, especially at Amiens and Lille. They were cheering and waving to us, and if we stopped some of the kids and the adults would climb up onto the tank. They threw flowers at us, and offered us food and drink, and in the evenings many of them invited us into their homes for a meal, although they didn't have much themselves; some even let us have a bath, which meant a lot to us.

During the fighting we did an awful lot of damage to some of the towns and villages, but to be fair, the people understood, and treated us very well. I think that they were just glad to be free again."

Finally, later on that evening, the order to stop for the night came, much to the relief of the shattered men. The regiment halted around the town of Assche, on the outskirts of Antwerp, and in a steady rain they ate some rations and tried to grab a few hours sleep before the next leg began in the morning. Although weary, they could be very satisfied with their work. Huge gains had been made over the last few days and Antwerp itself was now only a few miles away.

The advance made by the British was reflected by all of the other Allied forces, as no less than thirty Allied divisions had now crossed the River Seine. Twenty-First Army Group had driven deep into Belgium, and in doing so had cut off the German forces in the heavily defended garrisons around the channel ports; General Bradley's US Twelfth Army Group was making good progress towards Aachen, the first major city on the German border, and traditionally seen as the gateway to Germany; the US Third Army was racing towards Metz and Nancy in Eastern France; and a French-American force was advancing from the south into Alsace, again near the German border.

These rapid gains were an unexpected bonus, but they were tempered by the increasingly serious supply problem.

"You often hear about this fuel crisis, but to be fair I can only remember one time when we went short. A lorry with our fuel would never be far behind us, or now and again a tanker would turn up and we'd get our petrol from there. We'd all muck in with the fuelling. We'd

129

form a chain and pass these four-and-a-half gallon jerricans along until we were topped up.

Headquarters was called 'A Echelon' and was in the rear area a good few miles behind us, but all the fuel and supplies came from what was called 'B Echelon', which was only a couple of miles behind the line. That was like a mobile supply depot for the regiment, and if we needed fuel, equipment, clothing, or anything else for that matter, it used to come from there.

If we had a broken down vehicle it would go back to B Echelon to be sorted out. Our mail would be sent there too, and whenever somebody went back to B Echelon they'd collect the sacks and bring it up to the 'front' for us. It was always weeks behind but getting a letter was good for morale. My mam and dad used to write regularly, and I'd reply whenever I got the chance. My mam used to send five Woodbines in the envelope and by the time they'd get to me all the 'baccy' would have fallen out!

I had some cousins who were very good too. There was a scheme going in the national papers, the Daily Mail and so on, and if your family collected vouchers from the paper and then sent them in, they'd send cigarettes to the soldiers serving abroad.

Our troop was like a family; we shared everything. If you'd had a letter and your mate hadn't got one that time, you'd give him yours to read, and we'd show each other pictures of our wives or sweethearts. It kept us going. Partly because of censorship, but mainly because I didn't want to worry them, I never once mentioned how bad things were or the things I'd seen, but my dad had served in the Great War so he would have known what it was like. The only thing I did mention was later on when I met up with my brother, Fred.

My mam had already had a real fright a few months before. She'd bumped into a lad we'd known for years in Liverpool. He'd landed on Gold Beach on D-Day and been wounded, and now he was home on convalescent leave. I don't know what his motives were, but he was stupid enough to tell my mam how terrible it had been, and that he'd seen me on the beach. When I say that she went grey overnight I'm serious; she was sick with worry. You've got to remember that she had two of her lads over there, Fred and me.

I never met that bloke again and I think it's just as well."

As previously mentioned, the supplies for the Allied armies were still getting to the 'Front' over the Normandy beaches and through the port of Cherbourg, now over 300 miles in the rear. The enormous amount of supplies necessary to sustain the advance led to convoys of trucks, shuttling to and from the front, all day every day. Even these many hundreds of vehicles, each crammed with fuel, food, ammunition, and a multitude of other materiel, were not enough to alleviate the situation, especially on the American front to the south, and slowly but surely the advance began to run out of steam.

Antwerp was the key. This port, one of the largest in Europe, was now within striking distance for Montgomery's troops and Eisenhower and the other commanders were very anxious to bring it under their control. If it could be captured in fairly good condition, the supply difficulties would be eased, and planning for the coming winter campaign would be infinitely easier. In the vanguard of the assault on Antwerp would be the 11th Armoured Division, and at dawn on the 4th September the 86th was getting ready to protect the left flank of the 11th as the division moved towards its objective.

By mid-morning the regiment was in action south of the city and thanks in part to some assistance from the Belgian Resistance, the port was secured quickly and undamaged, the evacuating Germans not having had the time to sabotage the facilities. The unexpected ease of the port's capture was a surprise, albeit a nice one, to everyone concerned. For the next two days the regiment stayed south of Antwerp, at Willibroek, and supported a British attempt to cross the Albert Canal, which the Germans were using as a fixed defensive line.

On 7th September the 86th was given a critical order. Thirty miles away a British force had managed to establish a bridgehead over the Albert Canal at Beeringen and formations were being sent to consolidate the breakthrough, 11th Armoured

Division being one of them. This bridgehead was vital if the Allied advance was to continue, and as 11th Armoured raced to exploit the gain, the 86th Field Regiment was instructed to hold Antwerp until reinforcements arrived, probably around dawn on the 9th, a timeframe of about 36 hours.

With pockets of Germans still active in the surrounding area, and present in large numbers on the other side of the Scheldt, the estuary leading to the port itself, this was a crucial and hazardous task, especially for a single artillery regiment. Lt. Col. Fanshawe, recognizing this, deployed the unit's guns on the southern outskirts of the city, so that the entire area and its approaches were within range of the 25-pdrs. Spread thinly, 341 and 462 batteries were to guard the docks and the Albert Canal, while 342 Battery was given the task of defending the tunnel running underneath the estuary. Every man that could be spared from the guns was put into an infantry role, and any extra weapons were lent to willing members of the Belgian Resistance.

It was clearly stated that these positions must be kept out of German hands at all costs, and in a clever piece of subterfuge the unit was instructed to make as much noise as possible, and to fire at even the smallest target, in the hope that the Germans would be fooled into thinking that a much larger force was still present in the city.

"Antwerp was a nasty fight and I remember it got quite bad in the afternoon of the day we got there. Because we were the only ones there in the night the troop didn't stick to its usual positions. Instead of being in a

line like we normally would when firing, we were all over the place, firing at anything we could."

Fighting broke out several times during 8th September but Antwerp remained in British hands. During the afternoon, 342 Battery's commander, Major Kiln, was badly wounded in both legs during a German counterattack, which was beaten off. By the evening, reinforcements from 51st (Highland) Division had begun to arrive and the 86th could relax a little.

Having successfully defended the port, the regiment left the city the following day, and on the 10th crossed the Albert Canal at the Beeringen bridgehead. The performance of the regiment at Antwerp had been first-rate and now, stationed around the village of Kursaal, they were lucky enough to have a few 'quiet days'. Football matches against the locals, hot baths at the nearby pithead, and a handout of wine and cigarettes from a captured German train made it a very enjoyable time.

They had earned it. In less than a month since the breakout from Normandy, British Second Army had reached and crossed the Albert Canal. The Allies were unquestionably in the ascendancy and now, in an uncharacteristically bold and risky move, General Montgomery unveiled his plan to end the war by Christmas.

He called it Operation Market-Garden.

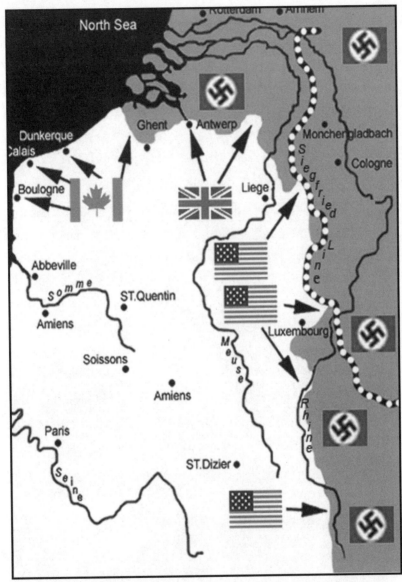

The Allied advance across France, September 1944

Mail reaches B Troop Command Post, July 1944

136

Major Kiln & the crew of X/342 at Bill-Montiny near Lille, 2nd September 1944

The seasoned warrior - Brussells 1944

Chapter Eight

The Gamble

17th September - 26th September 1944

During these heady days, of all the Allies gains, those made by the Second British Army were some of the most significant of the campaign. Since the breakout from the bridgehead at Vernon it had raced 250 miles through occupied territory and captured Amiens, Arras, Tournai, Brussels, Louvain and Antwerp - all key objectives in the overall plan.

Further, many of Eisenhower's original aims had been met. The flying-bomb facilities in Northern France had been captured and put out of action; the airfields in Belgium had been occupied, and a large port close to the front line, Antwerp, was now in Allied hands. However, having the largest port in Europe at your disposal is pointless if your ships cannot get to the docks, and this was exactly the situation that the Allies found themselves in, in September 1944.

The only seaward access to the port of Antwerp is via a fifty-mile stretch of estuary that links the port with the North Sea. This waterway, the Scheldt, is almost ten miles wide at its source, but tapers considerably near the port itself, and in 1944 it was heavily mined, with the now isolated German Fifteenth Army holding both banks. Any Allied ships attempting to use the port before the mines were removed or the banks cleared stood a good chance of being sunk without ever being able to deliver their much-needed cargo.

Eisenhower, was extremely frustrated by this situation, and his thinking was clearly influenced by it. His armies were hard on the heels of the enemy, but were now being forced to slow down due to a severe lack of fuel and supplies. To compound this problem, two of his more colourful commanders, Generals Montgomery and Patton, had taken to squabbling, each insisting that if allocated the remaining dwindling fuel supplies, their forces would overrun Germany in no time, and end the war by Christmas.

Montgomery, commander of the British and Canadian Twenty-First Army Group, had always advocated the 'single thrust' theory, believing that only by advancing en masse could the Allies completely break German resistance in the West. Eisenhower disagreed with this philosophy, preferring to attack all along the line, so that the enemy would be obliged to disperse their forces and not offer any defence in depth. Their differing ideologies were a constant source of friction between the two.

Montgomery, though, was nothing if not determined, and in the second week of September, he presented a plan to Eisenhower that surprised and tempted the Supreme Commander. Up until now 'Ike' had been committed to clearing the Germans from the Scheldt estuary, an action that would make Antwerp port operational, but after studying Montgomery's proposal he decided to gamble.

Brilliantly conceived and unusually daring, Operation Market-Garden offered an alternative route into Germany, and if successful, a genuine possibility of shortening the war significantly. In essence this bold plan had several key aims; to cut off the German forces in western Holland; to outflank the Siegfried line or Westwall - the formidable fixed defences along the German border - and to drive into the heavily defended Ruhr,

141

the industrial heartland of Germany. If the Ruhr could be reached and occupied the Germans' ability to wage war would crumble, perhaps in as little as three months; such was its importance to the Reich.

There was another good reason to take a chance on Monty's plan. From secret bases in Holland, the Germans had recently resumed launching the dreaded V2 rockets against Britain, and the death toll in the cities was mounting. During the Blitz of 1940–41 the British public had suffered terribly, and now four years later, between June and September, they had endured another deadly menace – the V1, or 'doodlebug' as it was grimly nicknamed. Over that period hundreds of these 'flying bombs' fell on London, causing over 21,000 civilian casualties, and forcing the population back into their shelters.

Fighter aircraft, massed anti-aircraft batteries, and eventually the capture of the launch sites in Northern France, all contributed to eliminating the hazard, but on 8th September the bombardment began again and this time the danger was even greater. The new weapon, the V2, contained a one-ton warhead and climbed seventy-five miles into the Earth's atmosphere before hurtling down on its target at four times the speed of sound. The height and velocity achieved by the weapon made it impervious to ground and air defences, and enabled it to hit its target with no warning; a terrifying psychological side-effect.

As the V2s began to rain down on London from their launch sites in Holland, pressure increased on Eisenhower to do something about them, which was another consideration that led him to give Monty the go-ahead.

With the Supreme Commander's blessing, Monty began briefing his staff on Operation Market-Garden. To an astonished audience the Field Marshall explained that the operation would be two-pronged, and consist of airborne and ground forces working very closely together. 'Market', the airborne part, consisted of three airborne divisions being dropped behind enemy lines in Holland. Once down, their primary objective would be to capture and hold open the key bridges between Eindhoven, and Arnhem, which lay on the south bank of the River Rhine 64 miles behind the German front line. With the bridges in Allied hands, the ground forces (the 'Garden' element) could travel along this airborne 'carpet' and fight their way through to Arnhem.

Speed would be the key. Montgomery believed that the airborne force could only hold out against the Germans for between 48 and 72 hours, so it was imperative the timetable was adhered to. The airborne troops, although superbly trained, would be lightly armed and have limited supplies. They would be depending on the ground forces getting to them fast, but that could only happen if they themselves could capture the bridges intact. Holland, with so much of its land criss-crossed by rivers and canals, is a country totally dependent on its many fine bridges, and in 1944 it was no different. The co-ordination and co-operation between the Market and Garden elements would need to be first class if the plan was to succeed, and failure at any stage would have a disastrous knock-on effect for the units ahead. In simple terms, it would be no use holding one bridge if the bridge before it had not been captured.

No one denied that the plan was, in theory, brilliant and highly imaginative, but many doubted that it could be carried out in practice. Because of the waterlogged countryside the Garden forces would have to advance along the only major road available (the Club Route as it was nicknamed), and this would make the thousands of vehicles involved vulnerable to ambushes and counterattacks.

Further, reconnaissance photos developed just prior to the attack clearly showed German tanks in Arnhem, including 20–30 'Tigers', when all intelligence reports had stated that the area was thinly defended by low-grade troops with poor equipment.

Most worrying of all though, especially for the commander of the airborne corps, Lt. Gen. 'Boy' Browning, was the strict timetable. He knew that if the Germans destroyed any of the bridges along the route before the ground forces could cross them, it would increase the strain on the troops at Arnhem. On studying the final plan Browning warned Montgomery, 'I think we may be going a bridge too far.'

Orders for Market Garden were given to XXX Corps units, including 86th Field Regiment on the 16th September, the day after they had arrived on the banks of the Meuse-Escaut Canal, near the border between Belgium and Holland. In essence, the priority for the regiment was to help keep the supply lines open along the Club Route. Each battery was to be attached to a squadron of the 15/19th Hussars, and together these armour-artillery groups would reinforce the US airborne forces, and form strong points along the route, repelling attacks from the flanks.

Of the three batteries, 341 would cross the Meuse Canal first, and head for Eindhoven. On arrival there, they were to link up with units of the US 101st Airborne Division (the Screaming Eagles) who would be approaching from the small town of Son, after capturing the bridge there.

Once 341 Battery had completed its task 342 Battery would leapfrog 341 and head for Veghel, to aid the paratroops in the defence of that bridge, and to keep the road open to Grave. 462 Battery would then move through 342 and move onto the bridge at Grave. No one was under any illusions regarding the importance of the task or of the difficulties involved, but morale was high and the men were confident.

> *"The bridgehead was absolutely choc-a-bloc with men and every type of vehicle you could imagine. It looked like an organised shambles. We were in a side field and after a bit of jostling and waiting we managed to get into position. I remember, not long after, a Stuka attacked the column, but the AA batteries drove it off.*
>
> *Our sergeant major gave us a bit of a briefing. He told us that it was a big op' and that we were making a dash for Arnhem, to get to the airborne troops that were going to capture the bridge there. That was it; the officers always knew more than us."*

September 17th dawned bright and sunny and in the bridgehead

145

on the Meuse-Escaut Canal the thousands of vehicles of General Horrocks's XXX Corps were waiting for the signal to advance, which could only be given when the ground forces knew that the airborne operation was under way. At around two o' clock that afternoon a gigantic armada of transport planes and gliders passed overhead, carrying the airborne troops to their objectives.

"What a sight! Anything that could tow a glider was in the air passing over our heads. The sky was full and the noise was deafening. It took hours for the armada to pass. Of course, the German flak batteries were pouring fire into them; you could see the tracers coming up from the ground and the planes falling out of the sky, on fire. As the fleet passed the canal they began dropping orange flares and that was our signal."

It was indeed, and almost at once 350 guns of the 86th and many other artillery units in the bridgehead began to pound the German position 400 yards in front of them.

"If I'm honest, I wasn't too worried about killing Germans at that point. Watching our planes crashing and all those lads being killed before they'd even had a chance, made me so angry that I didn't care."

With the shells whistling over their heads in a crescendo of noise, the leading tanks of XXX Corps revved their engines and moved off. The great gamble was under way, but it wasn't long before the fierceness of the German resistance became apparent. The first nine tanks were knocked out within 200 yards of each other, victims of well-concealed 88mm guns. The going was tough. Journeying through this marshy, heavily wooded countryside, infested with German infantry, was extremely dangerous and by dusk the leading tanks of XXX Corps had not yet reached Eindhoven. With the light failing they had no choice but to stop where they were, and a general halt was called. 342 Battery, still in the bridgehead area at the Meuse-Escaut Canal, had not moved at all and was now digging in for the night, during which a German counter-attack had to be repelled.

Despite the unexpectedly slow pace, due largely to the single road and the tenacity of the German defenders, the news wasn't all-bad. Up ahead, the Market elements had performed extremely well. In particular, the men of the British 1st Airborne Division, despite landing almost eight miles away from the bridge at Arnhem, had attacked the German garrison on the north bank and repulsed several counter attacks made against them. They had caught the Germans by surprise but they knew it wouldn't be long before they recovered and launched a major counterattack with heavy armour - something that the 'Red Devils' were distinctly lacking.

A cause for concern was the bridge at Son, or rather the lack of it. Caught unawares by the landings, the Germans had been forced to destroy the crossing just as the Americans were about to capture it. This was a bitter blow to the schedule, and the advance would be on hold until a Bailey bridge could be built. Another delay which would prove costly.

At first light on 18th September, the Guards Armoured Division continued their advance, and with the help of rocket-firing Typhoons, they broke through the German line and entered Eindhoven (to a rapturous welcome from the locals). As the leading tanks crawled through the streets, crowded with jubilant Dutch citizens, elements of the 101st Airborne Division, who had entered the town from the north around Son, greeted them and informed them of the blown bridge up ahead. Building materials were rushed forward and although the British engineers were masters of their art, it would take time to put the new bridge in place; time that the 'Garden' forces did not have.

Back at the canal the 86th still hadn't been able to get going, although 341 Battery had moved up to about 1000 yards ahead of its sister batteries. By now the advance had moved beyond the range of the regiment's guns but on the principle of never leaving guns idle they took on targets on the flanks of the advance.

It was a dangerous place to be. There were still hundreds of vehicles and guns in the bridgehead and during the evening of the 18th the Luftwaffe launched a heavy raid against the area with Junkers 88s. High explosive and armour-piercing bombs rained down on the men huddled in their slit trenches and vehicles, while the AA batteries fought desperately to bring the dive-bombers down. By the end of the raid several of the regiment's vehicles lay wrecked and burning, and Lt. Harry Dovey, the C.P.O. of 342 Battery had been killed whilst crossing the bridge to recce a new gun position for the battery.

After working through the night, the engineers of XXX Corps

had, by 06.15 on the 19th constructed a Bailey bridge over the Wilhelmina Canal at Son. The Guards Armoured Division began crossing immediately and within two hours some elements had raced 14 miles through Grave and made contact with troops of the US 82nd Airborne Division at Nijmegen. Now, advancing together, they fought their way towards the imposing road bridge that spanned the River Waal.

Although they were seriously behind schedule, XXX Corps had now negotiated over 50 of the proposed 64 miles to Arnhem and were at least able to engage the Germans around Arnhem with medium and heavy artillery at extreme range. The situation there was grim. Some reinforcements had arrived, including Polish paratroops that had suffered many casualties on their dropping zone, but they were not enough. The bad weather of the last two days had prevented most of the planes from the second and third airlifts from flying, and supplies that were being dropped were falling in to German hands; indeed, only 30 out of 400 tons had reached the beleaguered British troops by this point.

When news of the Guards Armoured Division's substantial leap had been confirmed it injected some much-needed impetus into the advance. Like many other units, the 86th received new orders; 341 Battery was moved up to near the bridge at Son in direct support of the Hussars, and was soon engaged in a fierce fight with six Panther tanks that were threatening the positions there. By the morning of the 20th all of the German tanks had been destroyed and the battery had made a major contribution to keeping the advance going in that area.

Actions like this were just about keeping Market Garden alive, but the operation was falling further and further behind schedule with each passing moment. By now the airborne troops at Arnhem were short of ammunition, food, water, medical supplies and other essentials, and were being forced into an ever shrinking pocket by heavy and regular attacks from German troops, some of which were Waffen-SS. Further, due to the failure of their radio sets they were to a great extent prevented from communicating with the Garden forces. As a result, the British soldiers fighting for their lives on the west bank of the Rhine were all asking themselves the same question, "Where are the tanks?"

The answer to that question could be found in the enormous traffic jam that now extended between the Meuse-Escaut Canal and Son. More often than not, the vehicles were stationary while enemy resistance from the flanks was dealt with by aircraft and artillery; and after every skirmish, blazing lorries, tanks, or other vehicles would have to be shunted off the road to clear a path for the remaining vehicles. For the tank crews and the gunners, never was the air superiority that the Allies enjoyed more welcome, for without the fighters casting their protective eye over them, these snaking columns of steel would be even more vulnerable than they already were.

This huge convoy moving along a single road over such flat terrain offered the defenders a tremendous target, and German units were appearing all along the tree-lined route, engaging the columns at close range with mortars, machine-guns, artillery and 'panzerfausts' – a hand-held, single shot, anti-tank weapon.

Although the sheer weight of the Allied forces would usually be enough to eliminate these individual threats, it took time, which meant further delays to the schedule.

By the evening of the 20th the enemy resistance in Nijmegen had been eliminated. The men of the 82nd Airborne had performed heroics by capturing the four crossings over the Waal River, including the enormous road bridge, the northern end of which they captured by making a daylight crossing of the river in assault boats, under heavy enemy fire. The leading tanks of the Guards Armoured Division had then rushed the bridge on the southern side and linked up with the Americans. The Allies were over the Waal and were now just 10 miles from their beleaguered comrades at Arnhem.

Word finally came for 342 Battery to move out on the morning of the 21st. Their orders were to bypass the endless line of traffic and head north to St. Oedenrode, a small town in between Son and Veghel. Attached to 44th Royal Tank Regiment, the battery was to give direct fire support as the struggle to keep the road open continued. As the Sextons started out, a steady rain began to fall, which would not stop for the remainder of the operation.

"When we finally did get going we made good progress. We got a tremendous welcome in Eindhoven, everybody did. The Dutch were great; they offered us all they had. They were thrilled to be liberated. I still write to some people out there.

Somewhere along the route we stopped for a bit and there was this Dutch Resistance bloke there who wanted his photo taken with us. He had one of those timer things on his camera, so he set it up, and he and his young son got in the middle of us with the tank behind, and we had our photo taken.

It was near Eindhoven that I met up with my brother. Imagine that! We were on stop by the side of the road and I noticed that some units of the 43rd Division were passing us. I sat there and asked a few blokes if they knew if the Duke of Cornwall's Light Infantry was nearby, but they weren't sure.

Well after a few hours I gave up and went back to my slit trench and had a cup of tea and a smoke. A bit later on I went back and tried again. This time I got lucky cos the D.C.L.I. happened to be going past. I says to this bloke 'Hey mate, do you know a fellow by the name of Sergeant Hamilton?' and he says 'Yes! He's up the road a bit in a carrier. In case you're wondering why Fred was Hamilton and I'm Kaye, it's because my mam had had Fred before she met my dad.

Anyway, I ran back as fast as I could to Sergeant Cooper and told him, and asked him if I could go up and try to see our Fred. Well he was great about it. He even got one of the lads to take me up the line in a motorbike and sidecar.

When I found our Fred he was dumbstruck! We were thrilled to see each other, but the best thing about it was that he was short of fags and money, and I still

152

had loads left over from our encounter with that German paymaster in Normandy. I gave him about a hundred fags and fifty guilders. He was really pleased he'd met me!

He was on his second tour of duty at that point. He'd not long come back from convalescent leave. He'd been wounded by splinters from a mortar bomb and even years later he was in and out of hospital, having bits of metal taken out of his body.

That wasn't the only time I met him in the war either; I met him later on too - in Germany."

Just prior to reaching St. Oedenrode, 342 Battery saw its first action of Market Garden, and within a few hours of arriving in the area worrying reports began to circulate. These messages stated that a German force of about 2,000 soldiers with one hundred 88mm guns was bearing down on the town in a flanking attack. If this wasn't bad enough, further reports brought even worse news; enemy armour was also approaching from the west and north, and a quick glance at the map was enough for the officers to appreciate the gravity of the situation.

The Germans were making an all-out attempt to cut the road through Veghel, which would mean that the Allied units that had already passed through on their way to Nijmegen and Arnhem would be isolated from the rest of XXX Corps, and surrounded by the enemy. The Germans were also aiming to blow up the four bridges in Veghel so that even if they had to withdraw, the Allies would not be able to cross the canal in strength for some time. They rightly assumed that if they could cut the supply line to the forces at Nijmegen, the much-needed reinforcements of men and armour there would stand little chance of breaking through to the stranded airborne troops at Arnhem.

In the German forces' way were the paratroops of the U.S. 101st Airborne, and elements of British armoured and infantry units. Hastily drawn-up plans for the defence were immediately put into action, which meant that despite having had little chance to rest, 342 Battery, with Major Whitmee now in command, spent the night firing 150 rounds into the German positions up ahead. This barrage harassed the enemy forces around Veghel and disrupted their efforts to mount a serious counter-attack against the bridge there.

The following morning, the 22nd, a new fire plan was given to the dog-tired men of 342. This time the battery was to support an attack by the 44th R.T.R.'s tanks, and infantry of the 'Screaming Eagles', as the battle to clear the route intensified. The fighting raged throughout the day, with the hard-pressed Allies just about managing to keep the road through Veghel open. Although being heavily shelled, 342 and an assortment of other batteries that had been taken off the road to join the battle pounded the Germans around Veghel, as the infantry and tank units of each side fought bitterly for control of the road and bridges.

As the battle unfolded the stream of Allied traffic heading north continued to cross the bridges, including the vehicles of 462 Battery, which had been called forward to a gun position southeast of Nijmegen. Almost immediately after 462 had moved just north of Veghel, the German attack finally succeeded in cutting the road there, and the scenario that the Allies dreaded most became a reality.

As darkness descended the fighting subsided, and the road remained closed. For the men of the 86th at St. Oedenrode, the day had involved answering call after call from the FOOs at Veghel, and by now they were tired and hungry, but at least they were alive. For the men of the 101st Airborne Division, the battle to keep open the Club Route was proving particularly costly and they soon christened the road with what they believed to be a more apt nickname - 'Hell's Highway'.

At dawn on the 23rd an armoured attack to reopen the road north of Veghel was put in by 44th RTR, supported by the batteries at St. Oedenrode, and assorted infantry units. Another day of heavy fighting ensued but by early evening the Allies had broken through the German cut in the road, and had made contact with elements of the Guards Armoured Division, that had turned south to attack the German line from the rear. Once again, the road was open for the Allied vehicles, but even as the units rolled out of Veghel everyone knew that time was running out for the troops at Arnhem.

By the following morning 342 Battery had moved up to a new position outside Veghel, and by lunchtime had lost three men (one killed) and a 25-pdr to enemy fire. Despite the casualties the battery kept going all day, putting down heavy fire on the enemy positions that flanked the Club Route. On top of this they continued to give valuable assistance to the American infantry at Veghel, who were under serious attack once again by German paratroops.

"We were under almost constant fire. The Germans had a 'spotter' in an OP [Observation Post] in a church and he was bringing down very accurate fire on us. They were using airbursts on us, the worst kind of fire to be under. The shells would explode at about head height and spray shrapnel in every direction. God help you if you were in the way of that stuff. We just put our helmets on, 'cwtched up' behind the tank as fast as possible, and prayed!

We tried and tried to knock that bloke out of the church tower, but we just couldn't manage to score a direct hit on it. It got to the point that we were shooting at anything that moved! You get immune to the killing, you just say to yourself 'Let's get it over with."

As darkness fell on the 24th, the men of 342 made a blood-curdling discovery. For some reason the infantry unit that had been in position around the battery during the last few days had moved out, leaving the battery on its own in a position that was definitely known to the enemy. By this point of the battle, patrols from both sides were infiltrating each other's positions almost at will, and the men knew that they were in for a long night.

"I thought they had us that night. The Germans were all along the route and I think that we were surrounded at one point. It was bloody frightening. We made for

Veghel and we had to be as quiet as possible because we didn't know if there were any Germans about.

The crossing was a drawbridge and portcullis effect if I remember rightly, and the Germans had it zeroed for artillery fire. We came out of the back lanes just before the bridge, and we had to time our crossing in between the bursts of shelling. As soon as the Americans lowered the bridge we sped through and crossed to safety. The paratroopers had kept a path open for us. Their officer got a Silver Star, I think.

I got on well with the Americans. I got pally with a Yank at Veghel, he was in the 101st Airborne. I gave him some English Oval cigarettes 'cos they loved our fags. It was around the time that we were cut off, and our units were near each other in a couple of fields. He was about the same age as me; he gave me his leg knife, which all the paratroopers had strapped to their boot. I've still got it.

I don't know whether he got out or not."

Enemy resistance along the whole 'corridor' had been effective and well organised from the outset, with mortar, artillery, and small-arms fire a constant threat to the Allied advance. Even now, nine days after the operation had begun the route was still under attack from German units that had again managed to cut the road, this time at a junction in a village between St. Oedenrode and Veghel. With 342 Battery in the thick of it again, it took yet another Allied infantry/armour attack before the

Germans were finally driven off, and for the road to be reopened.

> *"By the time the battle was over Veghel was knocked to hell. There were wrecked buildings and burning vehicles all over the town. It was a hell of a mess, some of the worst fighting we saw. We didn't know what was going on at Arnhem but we had heard that the Airborne were in trouble."*

Despite tremendous efforts by units of XXX Corps along the entire route, by the evening of the 25th time had run out for the men at Arnhem. As the bitter realisation of the operation's failure set in, the priority now was to extricate as many men as possible from the battle. Under the cover of a massed artillery barrage by the leading elements of XXX Corps, British and Canadian engineers evacuated the remnants of the British and Polish airborne troops from the north bank of the Rhine in assault boats mustered from units on the road. They left behind them a scene of desolation, and thousands of their comrades who were dead, dying, or too badly injured to be moved. Aside from the wounded, a further 6,000 British and 1,000 American troops went 'into the bag', swelling the POW cages that ran the length of central Germany.

The evacuation of the airborne troops signalled the end of Operation Market Garden. The ingenious attempt to outflank the WestWall [the German border version of the Atlantic Wall], in one leap had been foiled. Despite this, the Allies had managed to carve a fifty-mile corridor into German-occupied Holland,

and had crossed two of the three great rivers in front of the western German border.

Both sides had fought with tremendous courage and resilience during the campaign, but in the end General 'Boy' Browning's observation had shown itself to be accurate - Arnhem had proved to be 'a bridge too far'. More worrying for the Allies was the fact that the Germans had balanced the scales slightly. After their headlong flight from France they had now won an important battle, resulting in a much-needed boost to their morale.

For the Allies it had been an opportunity lost, and the optimistic hope that they would be home for Christmas quickly evaporated. In its place came the grim realisation that there was still a lot of ground to cover, and that the Germans, now settling in to positions along the length and breadth of the bristling Siegfried Line, would contest every inch of it.

It looked like being a long winter.

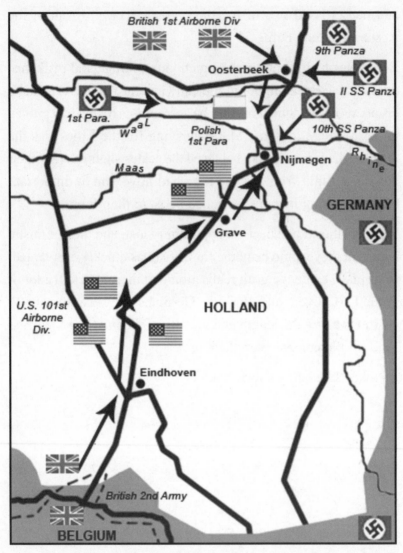

OP - Market Garden - the Allied attempt to outflank the Westwall

A postcard Ron acquired during Market Garden

Chapter Nine

Mud, sweat, and tears of joy

1st October - 17th December 1944

The failure of Market Garden brought the Allied commanders back down to earth with a bump. There would be no triumphant march into Berlin this year, or a lightning stroke that would end the war by Christmas. It was going to take time to break the Germans completely, and it was evident they were fighting as skilfully and savagely as ever.

The gloomy autumn of 1944 matched the mood of the Allied commanders and foot soldiers alike. The defeat at Arnhem had seen euphoria become shock and despair, and whatever the reasons for the setback, it had been a bitter pill to swallow after the summer victories. Now though, practicalities were the order of the day, and the task of preparing for the coming winter quickly re-focused the generals' minds.

One thing was clear; the offensive must be maintained. The Germans could not be allowed to rest for one moment, as they had already worked wonders in recent weeks by stabilising their Western Front. From D-Day to the middle of September they had lost 750,000 troops killed, wounded, or taken prisoner in Europe, and had been hard pressed on all fronts. However, reconstituted divisions from the Normandy campaign, had performed very well recently, and this reversal of fortune led the Germans to refer to this period as 'the miracle in the West'.

This new army, the Volksturm or 'people's army' was mainly made up of youths, older men, and recovering troops, but was still a force to be reckoned with despite its shortcomings in training and equipment. What they lacked in materials its members made up for in spirit and grim determination; the sacred soil of the Fatherland itself was now under threat, and many were prepared to die to protect it. The war was about to enter a new phase.

These troops, along with the dreaded SS divisions, spread out through the multitude of bunkers and fortified villages that made up the Westwall, and readied themselves to repel any Allied attempt to set foot on German ground. It was going to be a battle of attrition, a fight to the finish, and despite the Allies' material advantages, the outcome was anything but clear.

The weeks following the Arnhem debacle saw the Allies getting back to basics, in an attempt to 'tidy up the line'. Their combined armies now stretched from 'the island' in the north - the area between Nijmegen and Arnhem - right down to the Swiss frontier, a front of approximately 300 miles. In the north, the left flank, the opening of the port at Antwerp now became the main objective. The docks, although in Allied hands for over a month, lay idle and would continue to do so until the Germans were cleared from the west bank of the Scheldt Estuary - a task allocated to the First Canadian Army.

While the Canadians battled through the marshy lowlands in the north, British Second Army was ordered to turn east and head for the northern section of the Ruhr region. This critically important iron and steel centre of Germany was bristling with defences of every type, sitting as it did in the very heart of the Siegfried Line. The difficulty in penetrating the Ruhr Valley was blatantly clear - the Germans would defend this area to the last man and the last round, but if Germany was to be defeated there was no other way.

About 100 miles south of Arnhem, a joint British and American operation was being planned. The US Ninth Army now stood shoulder to shoulder with the right wing of British Second Army, which was at this point advancing on the city of Cologne. Before the war, Cologne had been an important cultural centre and was renowned for its handsome architecture, but now at the end of 1944, it had become a sprawling mass of rubble - a consequence of the Strategic Bombing Offensive waged by the air arms of the Allied forces.

Despite its ruined state, Cologne was a major objective for the British, as it lay on the last natural barrier to the Allied advance – the Rhine. However, before anyone could even think as far ahead as Cologne, the road network leading to it would need to be captured and secured, and the hub of that network lay in the small German town of Geilenkirchen.

Situated approximately 30 miles west of Cologne, Geilenkirchen and the surrounding villages were the key to the advance, and the amount of men and materiel dedicated to the operation reflected their strategic importance. Once again the Guards Armoured Division of XXX Corps would bring their tanks into the fray, where they would be joined by the infantry of the British 43rd Division, and the US 84th Division, the 'Railsplitters' as they were known. Further, some of Hobart's Funnies had been brought in to beat paths through the numerous minefields. As usual, the assault would be preceded by a devastating aerial bombardment, this time by 1,200 Flying Fortresses.

The aim of the operation, 'Clipper', was for the infantry of each division to skirt around Geilenkirchen, cut it off by encircling it, and to then secure the heights and villages in the immediate area. Once this had been done the US infantry was to enter the town itself and destroy the German forces present. A particularly important objective of the attack was the bridge at the village of Linnich, eight miles east of Geilenkirchen. If this crossing could be captured intact the Allies could gain a foothold over the Roer River, which would remove another obstacle in the advance to Cologne.

Like most plans it sounded straightforward, but the 'Railsplitters' were not so naïve as to believe anything other than that they were in for a tough time. Unlike the battle-hardened British 43rd Division, this was to be their first taste of combat, and supported by British 8 Armoured Brigade with 86th Field Regiment under command, they would be advancing on the most potent stretch of the infamous 'Siegfried Line'. The attack was scheduled for 15th November.

Since the end of Market Garden on 26th September the gunners of the 86th had continued to support the 82nd Airborne Division near Nijmegen. The Germans had continued to counter-attack the Allied positions in that area, and the regiment had been kept very busy supporting their American comrades, who had come to trust and rely on them. Danger was ever-present in the newly won corridor. The physical and mental tiredness could not be endured indefinitely, so it was not a moment too soon when the regiment was pulled out of the line on 12th October, for a rest and maintenance period.

"It was around that time that I got my hands on a 48hr pass to Brussells. We went to a little place just outside the city, called Zeekum. Peter and me headed straight for the nearest hair salon; we found one in this little square with all kinds of shops. We had a haircut, a shampoo, and we had all the dirt scraped out from under our fingernails! It was impossible to keep them clean in the line. It was while we were in Zeekum that we first saw the flying bombs going overhead on their way to Antwerp.

There was a little café in the square and the girl that ran it did portraits as well. It was there that John and I had our portraits done; I've still got the photo. Whenever I think of Zeekum and that café, it immediately reminds me of the Joe Loss song, 'Jealousy'. It was on a lot."

The trip was a welcome diversion for the men after recent events. During Market Garden the regiment had covered itself in glory, and letters from the commander of the 82nd US Airborne Division to General Dempsey of British Second Army, highlighted the tremendous performance of the regiment. The heavy and extremely accurate fire that the gunners had laid down during the battle had saved many American lives, and it had not gone unnoticed. For the masterful way that Lt. Col. Fanshawe had organised the regiment's guns he received the Distinguished Service Order.

Now though, the men were looking forward to a well-earned

break. On the day they left the Americans they once again became part of XXX Corps, as they had been transferred to the Guards Armoured Division, with whom they immediately moved into a 'rest and maintenance' camp near Grave. Although the men had performed heroics during the last few months the drill-sergeant at the camp soon had them thinking they were back in Basic Training.

"To be honest I can't remember a lot about the barracks, but I do know that they were in a pretty poor state. I don't think we even had lights [the Germans still held the nearby power station.] We thought we were going in for a bit of a rest but it didn't turn out like that. We spent a lot of the time cleaning the tank up, 'cos it had weeks of mud stuck to it.

On top of that we had all our kit and other equipment to clean, cos we also had to do drill, and marching, and PT. We thought that was a bit unfair considering what we'd been through since June, but we had no choice – we had to do it. I remember one night we'd gone for a visit to Nijmegen. Before we came back we stopped to have a bite to eat in the canteen. Anyway, this night, I was outside with my mate John waiting to get in, when a German shell landed right on the place. There was a hell of a mess, people killed and wounded."

On 5th November, after three weeks at the camp, orders to move out came through. Within two hours the tanks and trucks of the regiment were packed up and ready to roll, and they soon began a journey to an area 40 miles south east of Grave. After a few days of stopping and starting the regiment came into action near the Dutch-German border, around the villages of Born, Guttekoven and Einighausen.

"During the few days we had at Guttekoven we were billeted with a Dutch family, Tummers I think their name was. The fighting was going on away from the village so the civilians were still in their homes, and if you could sort it out for yourself, you could find 'civvy billets'. Well, Peter and I both stayed with the same family and we got on great with them; there were a lot of them too! As well as the parents there was six brothers and four sisters, and I ended up knocking one of the sisters off; Ann her name was. She was lovely.

While we were there they had a party for Wilhelmina, the youngest child cos it was her birthday. By this point in the war they didn't have much and they could only manage a little black cake with an old candle for her. I thought to myself 'what a way for a kid to spend her birthday', so I went to our cook and I said 'Hey mate, we've got a kiddie down here with bugger all for her birthday, have you got anything spare going?

Fair play, he give me some scones and stuff and as I was walking back I said to myself 'Oh bugger it', and off I went to our tank."

During the race through Belgium the regiment had passed by

many towns and villages whose shops had been 'liberated' by either the advancing Allies or the retreating Germans. Indeed, the men of the regiment were not shy themselves when the opportunity presented itself.

> *"I got a lovely doll from an empty shop in Belgium, everybody was taking things, so I just picked it up and thought, 'I'll have this.' I took it for my little sister, and it was lovely. It cried, everything, a real proper doll. I stored it in one of the empty ammunition cases that we had on the tank, and it came right through Holland with me. I was looking forward to giving it to my sister when I got home."*

Now though, Ron was on a mission to make another little girl's birthday a bit special.

> *"I got the doll from the tank, took it back to the party and gave it to Wilhelmina. Well, when she saw it she cried, I cried, everybody in the room cried I think! It made her day!*
>
> *Another thing I remember about that day was when I offered the father, I think he worked in the local electrical plant, some tobacco for his little pipe, cos he was putting leaves or something in it, just to be able to have a smoke.*
>
> *We had bags of bloody tobacco so I went to get a bit to give him some. Well, his face lit up! And then he goes in the cupboard and gets a bloody pipe that looked like a bucket on the end of a broomstick! My can of tobacco*

just disappeared! We laughed like hell about it.

There was a lad at Guttekoven who I met again years later. He told me about the time that he'd been horse riding in a field near to where we were firing, and that the blast had lifted him out of his saddle! Do you know, he was only nine or ten at the time, but all those years later when we met again, he still remembered the numbers on our tank, except that he thought they were 4711, instead of 1147.

He was the one who helped me find Wilhelmina all those years later when I went back. I met up with him in the village and I explained who I was looking for, and after we'd had a drink together and a look through my photos, he told me to wait where I was while he went to see what he could find out. Well, when he came back he had good news. He'd found Wilhelmina and offered to take me to her new address. Her name was Mrs. Orion now, her married name. So off we went, there were eight of us!

We knocked on her door and this bloke explained to her that I was Ron, and that I'd been there during the war. Well, she invited us in, but I don't think that she remembered me until someone called me Ron (Ron has been universally known as Danny since the 1950's). Well, as soon as she heard that she said RON! RON! MY DOLL!

She still had it, well, one of her grandchildren did. She

172

was thrilled! She got straight on the phone to her sister Ann, who I'd had a bit of a thing with at that time, but she pretended not to remember me. She KNEW all right!

We had a great time there. Do you know, whenever I used to go into the house I'd take my boots off outside, and when I would go to get them again, they'd always been cleaned.

Years later when I went back with my missus, we got treated like royalty. When we went out for a meal, we had the best service, and our hotel bill was paid for us. The Dutch were genuinely grateful at the time, and still are. We were sorry to leave that place in 1944 but a couple of weeks after we left we had to go back anyway cos the Germans had recaptured the village from the Americans that replaced our division."

As these events were unfolding, the final preparations for Operation Clipper were being made. The staff work and planning was of the usual British thoroughness, and they needed to be because in between the soldiers and their objectives stood some of the most formidable defensive positions ever constructed.

The Westwall (Siegfried Line to the British) was a three-mile-deep set of fortifications that ran the length of Germany's western border. Built in the thirties, the pillboxes, 'dragon's teeth', command posts, and troop shelters had lain unused and gathering dust while the German Army swept all before it.

However, this was now 1944 and things were different; the wolf was almost at the door and Hitler quickly ordered the complex to be the focal point of the German defence. Its big test was imminent – could it hold the Allies? Around Geilenkirchen, the troops of both sides were about to find out.

At dawn on 18th November the guns of the British and American artillery shattered the early morning air, as the assault got under way in appalling conditions. The weight of the bombardment was staggering, with 342 Battery alone firing 400 rounds of high explosive per gun into the German lines. Already suffering from the air onslaught, the barrage left the Germans reeling and by midday the infantry had gained good ground. It was a case of so far so good for the Allies but the weather was now starting to seriously impede them. Sucking mud made every footstep a struggle and even the tanks suffered, as their narrow tracks could not negotiate the sodden terrain.

Further, as the assault continued, the bunkers and pillboxes of the Siegfried Line came into play, and along with these defences the added threat of minefields, booby-traps and 'hull-down' panzers had to be considered. In the relentless downpour bitter fighting ensued, and casualties began to mount on both sides.

Despite their inexperience and high casualties the 'Railsplitters' were fighting well, and by the following day they had linked up with their British counterparts on the east side of Geilenkirchen, completing the encirclement of the town. They were understandably proud of their accomplishment but unfortunately this would be the highpoint of the operation. That night the weather deteriorated further, and for the next four days the gunners, tank crews, and infantry of both sides slugged it out in just about the worst conditions imaginable this side of the Russian Front.

"Everything was against us; the mud, rain, cold, everything. We were being shelled day and night, especially from airbursts. I had a very narrow escape one day there. I was sitting on the toilet, we used to dig a pit away from the gun and hang a canvas sheet around it, when a shell landed close by. It blew the canvas away like it wasn't there! I had such a fright that I just ran off with my pants around my ankles! I was very lucky.

When you're firing day and night, taking fire yourself, in the cold and the mud and the rain, it's bloody miserable, but you have to manage. If we had ten minutes spare someone would put a brew on, and if there was no field kitchen we'd just manage with our 'billy cans', these 12 or 24 hour packs that would keep you going.

Trying to stay dry was impossible, your clothes would just dry on you. I used to wear my 'denims' as much as possible cos they didn't hold the rain like the BD's.

We got really knocked about at Geilenkirchen. We took the place, but it was a bloodbath."

By 23rd November the battlefield was little more than a sea of mud, reminiscent of the Flanders battles of the First World War.

Allied infantry attacks north of Geilenkirchen were meeting stout resistance from the 10th SS Panzer Division, the victors of Arnhem, and movement of any kind became a struggle not only against a determined foe, but also against the horrendous conditions. By this point the men were exhausted, especially the infantry. They were low on ammunition, soaked through, cold, tired, and in desperate need of hot food. It was with enormous relief to everyone when they were pulled back and the attack was called off later that day.

As the shattered troops went back to their water-filled foxholes and slit trenches, the Allied commanders considered the events of the last five days. True, 'Clipper' had not achieved all of the objectives set, but Geilenkirchen had been taken. No one could deny that it was another step in the right direction, but as the depleted ranks of the 43rd and 84th divisions clearly showed, it had not been without cost.

For the men of the 86th it had been as miserable a time as they could remember. Doubtless, if they had been told that conditions were about to get worse they would have scoffed at the idea. At that point in their army career few of them had even heard of the Ardennes, but between now and the end of the year events would unfold which would ensure that it would be a place they would never forget.

Anne from Guttekoven

In the Reichswald Forest, Feb 1945
Ron is on the left.

Chapter Ten

Wrong place, wrong time

25th November - 17th December 1944

Although the Ardennes conflict was fought on an immense scale, for the sake of this account I have broken it down into three parts; the initial German assault, the Allied success in stabilising the situation, and ultimately the Allied counterattack. It is a very simplified version of events, but it is sufficient to illustrate the role that 86th Field Regiment played in one of the largest land battles of the conflict.

On 24th November the 86th returned to the positions they had occupied before the Geilenkirchen operation. The men were in desperate need of fresh clothes, hot food, and above all, sleep. For the first two days at Guttekoven, they were given complete rest, and for ten days afterwards the regiment occupied a defensive position that required very little artillery support.

To a man they were exhausted. Geilenkirchen had sapped the last reserves from their weary bodies, and now, all they wanted was a bit of piece and quiet and a spell out of harm's way. Their dishevelled appearance however, belied the regiment's standing. These men that had come off the line caked in mud and soaking wet, were by this point as good at what they did as any regiment in the Royal Artillery. Once again their outstanding performance in recent action had been singled out for praise; on the recommendation of the commanding general of the 84th US Infantry Division Lt. Col. Fanshawe was awarded the US Legion of Merit, and two members of 341 Battery also received American decorations.

As nice as this recognition was, for many the most memorable aspect of the stay at Guttekoven was the introduction of the 'zoot suit'. The winters in northwest Europe could be extreme and when the cold weather clothing finally arrived it was more than welcome.

"Thank God we got those suits when we did! Not everybody got them mind, just the blokes with the outdoor jobs. They were one piece, with a zip up front, and they were lined on the inside with fur. They really kept you warm.

Monty gave us permission to wear them home, and much later when I did eventually manage to get home on leave from Verden, I wore mine. I got off at the train station in Liverpool, and this 'redcap' came up to me and said, 'You're improperly dressed!' How do you make that out? I said. 'That's not regimental uniform,' he said, 'I know,' I said, 'I've just come home on leave and Monty's given us permission to wear them.' 'You're not allowed to wear it in England!' he said.

Well by this point I was getting a bit fed up with this bloke so I said to him, 'what are you going to do about it? I hope you're going to put me in that lock-up for six months, cos if you like, you can take my place over there!'

He just let me go!"

By 6th December the regiment was well rested and had recovered from its recent ordeal, but it was again pulled out of the line, this time for essential maintenance. It was thought that another major offensive was being planned for the near future, and that the terrain over which the Sextons would be operating would not be favourable. Therefore, for the next ten days, at a small village near the town of Sittard, twelve miles west of Geilenkirchen, the crews spent their time fitting special shoes to the tracks of their vehicles.

This period away from the line was very welcome, but the men were experienced enough to realise that it would not last long, and sure enough, on 17th December they were told to be ready to move at a moment's notice. Having received orders like this many times before, they had no reason to suspect anything out of the ordinary, but the 'top brass' knew better. South of the regiment's position, on the border between southern Belgium and Germany, there had been a major development.

For Adolf Hitler, the counter-offensive in the Ardennes, (or the 'Battle of the Bulge' to the Allies because of the bulge it created in the US line), was a last throw of the dice. His enemies were slowly but surely advancing from all angles into the territories of the Reich, and he knew that time was running out. The resources at his disposal were dwindling rapidly, and he knew that unless he made a determined strike against the western Allies soon, they would overrun Germany within months. Intelligence reports had also shown that the Russians were planning to launch a massive offensive in the near future.

For months, Hitler had considered how and where to land the blow, before finally settling on the Ardennes region, the starting point for his western Blitzkrieg in 1940. Despite the events of that year the Allies had not learned their lesson, and inexplicably, still believed this heavily-wooded, semi-mountainous region to be totally unsuitable for a large armoured thrust. Hitler knew this, and was quick to exploit it. The plan was undoubtedly cunning. The Allies had become over-confident, and they had over-stretched their supply lines. By attacking where he intended to, he could strike a stunning blow before they had time to react.

The main aim of the plan was for his armies to breakout of the Ardennes, and slice through the American front at its weakest point, a sixty-mile stretch between Monschau, and Echternach, that had been so quiet recently that it was known as the 'ghost front'. Once the Allied line had been pierced, the panzers and mechanised infantry would swarm through, cross the River Meuse, and head for the port of Antwerp, 125 miles away to the north.

If that city could be reached and occupied, the Allies would once again be deprived of a major port, which would affect their operational capabilities in the coming winter. Hitler also hoped that it would place even greater strain on the Anglo-American relationship, already frosty after the Market-Garden campaign. Further, creating a physical wedge between the Americans and the British would isolate the latter of the two, and force them to halt all offensive operations for some time. It was an ambitious plan but by this point Hitler's powers of reason were deserting him. He still believed that Germany was destined for victory, and it was this ideology that shaped the ambitious objectives of the plan.

Surprise would be vital. The Allies must remain confident that Germany was incapable of launching a major offensive, so all of

183

the build up was conducted in absolute secrecy. In a forest connected to the Ardennes, hidden from the prying eyes of the Allied planes, a fearsome arsenal was being assembled. During November and December, 240,000 troops, 1,000 tanks (including 90 of the new 68-ton King Tigers), 4.2 million gallons of petrol, and no less that fifty trainloads of ammunition arrived during the hours of darkness.

The only sticking point was the Allies unquestioned dominance of the skies. As a result, Hitler timed the assault to coincide with what he hoped would be a period of bad weather. If the Allied aircraft could be kept grounded, the assault stood a much better chance of succeeding. On studying the plan many of Hitler's senior commanders were flabbergasted by its objectives, and they were not slow to say so. Hitler however, was adamant; the attack would go ahead and soon; only he and the weather would decide when.

The time duly arrived at 05.30 on the morning of 16th December. In the freezing conditions fourteen infantry and eleven panzer divisions smashed into the thinly held US line along the 'ghost front'. The savagery and swiftness of the assault stunned the defenders unfortunate enough to be in its path, and a sizeable retreat was soon underway. To compound the panic and the confusion in the Allied lines, about 2,000 English-speaking German commandos were now on the loose behind enemy lines. Dressed in US uniforms, and led by Otto Skorseny, the man who had rescued Mussolini, they began to spread misinformation, switch road signs at important junctions and sabotage US equipment.

Despite some courageous resistance, the assault quickly overran the forward areas, but two telling stands by American forces would be made in the next few days, which would force the Germans to alter their plan. On 17th December, units of the sixth Panzer Army advanced on the town of St Vith, about 40 miles directly south of Aachen, and a major road and rail link to Germany. If they could capture St Vith, supplies could be carried forward by train directly to the most advanced formations of the German spearhead. This was a crucial objective because the German supply situation was in a critical state, making it imperative that St Vith fell quickly.

The plan was for the town to be in their hands by 6pm on the opening day, but standing in the path of 'Sepp' Dietrich's panzers were the men and tanks of the US 7th Armoured and 106th Infantry Divisions. Desperate fighting ensued, and despite furious efforts, the Germans were forced to seek a route around the town, an act that cost them precious time. It was not until 21st December that St Vith was captured by the Germans - four days too late.

As news of the offensive reached Eisenhower, he initially concluded that it was a local attack. However, as more and more reports reached his headquarters, the gravity of the situation became apparent, and his actions were decisive. Within four days 200,000 Allied troops were on their way to the Ardennes to reinforce the line. Away to the north, on the afternoon of the 20th, the men of the 86th were preparing to move into billets in the village of Rhode-St-Pierre, near Louvain, fifteen miles east of Brussels. News came that the move was cancelled and that the regiment should leave for the Ardennes immediately, along with the Guards Armoured Division, to join the growing battle.

"Well as usual we weren't told the ins and outs of what was going on, just that we were moving out. I was really fed up because I was meant to be going home on leave at that point. I was packed and everything, all dressed up in my best BDs I was just waiting for the truck to come and pick me and a few other lads up to take us back to A Echelon. I was that close to missing it all.

I was just unlucky I suppose, but looking back it was probably for the best, because going home on leave half way through the campaign, and knowing that you'd be going back into battle when you returned would have been harder to take, I think. I know that my brother, our Fred, was very dejected when it happened to him.

Thinking about it, I didn't have any leave at all. I went right through from D-Day to Verden without going home once."

The icy weather and poor visibility contrived to make the journey slow and tiring, but by the morning of the 21st, the regiment had arrived in the village of Hakendover, 12 miles to the southeast of their starting point. The division had been allocated an area between the nearby towns of Huy and Namur, on the banks of the Meuse, where it was ordered to stand fast against any German attempt to cross the waterway in that area.

"The thing that got me was that on our way to our gun positions where we were to make a stand, we were travelling through this American unit's sector, and as we were driving to the 'front' they were marching away from it, past where we'd come from! To top it all off, they were waving to us as we passed!"

Many troops arriving at the front had similar experiences. Although it is true that there were desertions in the US ranks, it is also true that most stayed to do their duty against overwhelming odds. The sheer weight of the German attack had caused panic on an unprecedented scale and some US outfits simply ceased to function. As they headed towards the battle, the German advance wasn't the only thing on the minds of the gunners. Christmas day was fast approaching and they were eager to find decent billets in which to have their dinner that day. Existing as they had over the last few months, sleeping rough and living on whatever food was available, the prospect of a proper cooked dinner had attained almost mythical status. Now, by chance, it looked as if they were going to be staying in Hakendover over the festive period, which meant that preparations for the big day could begin in earnest.

"We pulled out all the stops; everyone pitched in. In between our stints at the guns we made a real effort. There was a school in the village and we did it out lovely. We'd collected all sorts for the dinner, from all sorts of places! We'd even found some decent plates and cutlery. We were really looking forward to a good feed."

187

Despite all of the hard work put in by the men to make Christmas Day as normal as possible, the illusion was quickly shattered. The military situation had not improved and on 24th December the regiment's batteries were split up. 462 and 341 batteries left to join their allocated units, while 342 Battery was sent to the town of Givet, about 50 miles to the south, where it was to support the 23rd Hussars.

> *"Well now I was really fed up! Not only had I missed my leave, now I was going to miss my Christmas dinner as well! We just had to leave everything where it was. We left Hakendover at about four o'clock in the morning, and even though it was snowing like mad, the woman and her two kids from the house we were billeted in, came to see us off. Standing in the lane in the pitch black, freezing cold, knowing you were going back into battle, and gonna miss out on the only decent meal you'd had in weeks, meant morale was really bad."*

By Christmas morning, in the biting cold and heavy snow, the men of the regiment had joined with their latest partners and had begun crossing the mighty River Meuse. They then moved 10 miles east to Beauraing, where they had again been ordered to form a defensive position. Unlike 341 Battery, which had been involved in some heavy fighting in their area since Christmas Day, the men of 342 were lucky enough to spend the next few days out of the action, as no German attack had reached them yet, but the arctic conditions of their surroundings precluded any real appreciation of this quiet time, as everyone was too busy making sure they didn't freeze to death.

They had been cold before, but this was different. The icy wind and thick blanket of snow made life very difficult with daytime temperatures never rising above freezing, and the nights plummeting to a crippling –20 degrees. It didn't get light until eight in the morning, and it was dark again by 4.30 in the afternoon. A more depressing place to spend the festive period is difficult to imagine, but on 27th December, in these pitiless conditions, the men ate their Christmas Dinner - no decorations, no fun, and more importantly, no heat.

"Bully beef and biscuits; that's what I had for my Christmas dinner in 1944! I wasn't very happy at all. Without a doubt, It was the coldest place that I've ever been to, and being on the tank, which was all steel, made it even worse. Even with our 'zoot suits' on the cold still got through. If you weren't on the gun firing, or on maintenance duty, you'd just get in your slit trench and try to get a bit of warmth going. What made it worse was I wasn't even meant to be there.

Mind you, digging the trench was no mean feat, 'cos the ground was like rock. I remember we passed by a Scottish regiment that was digging in at the sides of a road, so they could ambush the Germans as they passed. Well, even though it was freezing, the ground was so hard that these lads were stripped to their vests with the sweat pouring out of them.

One good memory I've got from around that time was

when we passed through this little village called Wellin. I had a good mate in our troop called Dusty Wellin, who drove our ammunition truck. As soon as he saw the village sign he made sure that he had his photo taken by it. I've still got that photo." [Dusty Wellin attended 86th Field Regiment's reunions for years after the war, and Ron was always thrilled to see him. Sadly, in June 2003 Ron received word that Dusty had recently passed away.]

As the New Year dawned the tide was slowly turning in the Allies' favour. Since Christmas Day visibility had improved, and the heavy fog that had kept the Allied aircraft grounded had given way to relatively clear skies. With the outcome of the battle still delicately balanced, this was a critical factor, and the Allied air commanders wasted no time in getting the Typhoons and bombers into the air.

"That was a lovely Christmas feeling! Seeing our planes in the skies again gave everyone a bit of a lift. It was the first time that we'd been without air cover since we'd started and you noticed it.

A typical day for us in the Ardennes saw us moving around a lot, giving fire support to any unit that needed it. When you think that every field and road was covered with snow and ice, you can get some idea of how difficult it was for our vehicles to get about.

It was a hell of a job sometimes, especially going up and down hills. We'd throw all sorts under the tracks of the tanks so that we could get a bit of grip, but many a time it would make no difference and the tank would just slide sideways down the road into a ditch.

We had this big Scammel truck that followed our tanks around, and it had all sorts of equipment on it. It was able to plant itself in the snow and winch a tank or a lorry out if they got stuck, which they very often did."

By the end of the month the pulverising firepower of the air forces, and the grim determination of the US defenders at Bastogne, (a vitally important road junction that had been surrounded for days until General Patton's army broke through), and other points along the line, had brought the German advance to a standstill. Now, low on ammunition and with their gas-guzzling panzers almost out of fuel, they realised that the assault had petered out.

The attack had not been without success - some units had penetrated the Allied lines to a depth of sixty miles on a thirty-mile front, but this was to be the pinnacle of their achievements. The remainder of the battle would see the Germans retreating east, and being subjected to attacks on all sides of the 'bulge', which they themselves had created.

Now that the initial panic had subsided and the line had been stabilised, the Allies saw an opportunity to launch a major counterattack from both north and the south. By now the British 6th Airborne Division had been rushed in by land from England, and moved into the area already thinly held by 29 Armoured Brigade, which the 86th was attached to at that moment. In the

Arctic conditions the Allied forces prepared to push back the 'bulge' and straighten their line.

Locally the 2nd Fife and Forfar Yeomanry, and the 7th and 13th Parachute Battalions, with the 86th in direct support, was to capture the villages of Bure and Wavreille, which were about 25 miles northwest of Bastogne. They were also instructed to exploit any further opportunities that presented themselves.

On 3rd January the attack was launched. The German troops in Bure were well supported by a number of Tiger tanks, and the fighting quickly developed into a desperate struggle, house-to-house, and hand-to-hand in some cases. With the Sextons of 342 Battery laying down devastating defensive fire, which broke up many German counter-attacks before they could gather momentum, the airborne troops held the village until 6th January, at which time the battalion was brought out of the line.

13th Para had suffered 189 casualties in two days, but the battalion's commander had been so impressed with 342 Battery's performance during the battle that he recommended Major Whitmee, successfully, as it later transpired, for the Military Cross. The citation contains a tribute to the 'quite exceptional' fire support provided by the battery.

Aside from the heavy fighting, Ron's memories of that period are dominated by one thing - the weather.

"My abiding memory of that time isn't the long hours at the guns, or being under fire; it was the cold. It even affected our sleep. I mean we never got a lot of kip anyway, but out there you couldn't sleep; it was just

too cold. On occasion you'd be so exhausted that
you'd just sleep a 'dead man's sleep', or other times
you'd manage to have a nap for an hour or so. It was
hard, but you managed; you had to."

By 8th January, the Germans were retreating everywhere to the relative safety of the Siegfried Line. As they went, the Allies harassed them at every opportunity and the 'bulge' in the American line began to disappear, as large parts of territory that the Germans had overrun at the start of the offensive once again fell into Allied hands.

By 16th January the regiment's role in the 'Battle of the Bulge' was complete and it headed for Diest, thirty miles from Brussels, for rest and maintenance. Sporadic fighting continued across the whole front for another two weeks, with St.Vith being recaptured by the Americans on 23rd January, but in essence the battle in the Ardennes was over, and like Arnhem for the Allies, it had proved a costly gamble for the Germans.

The scale of the battle had been colossal. Approximately one million men had been involved in the struggle, which saw more Americans engaged than in the battle of Gettysburg in 1865. The Germans had inflicted 81,000 casualties on the Allies, but they themselves had come off even worse. By the middle of January they had been pushed back to the starting point of the attack and had suffered appallingly. 100,000 troops, and 2,000 tanks and planes had been lost - men and materiel that their virtually destroyed homeland could not replace. To compound these losses, the Russians had launched an enormous offensive in the east on12th January, made up of over 2,000,000 men, 7,000 tanks, and 46,000 pieces of artillery.

By now, the Thousand Year Reich was in its death throes, but Hitler refused to admit it. He would allow the bloodletting to continue until either Germany or the enemy was destroyed. For the troops on the ground, it would mean months more of suffering and hardship.

The battle would have to be taken into the heart of Germany; right to the fuhrer's door if necessary, but before that could happen there was the small matter of piercing the westwall, and negotiating a crossing over the Rhine, one of Europe's largest and most heavily defended rivers.

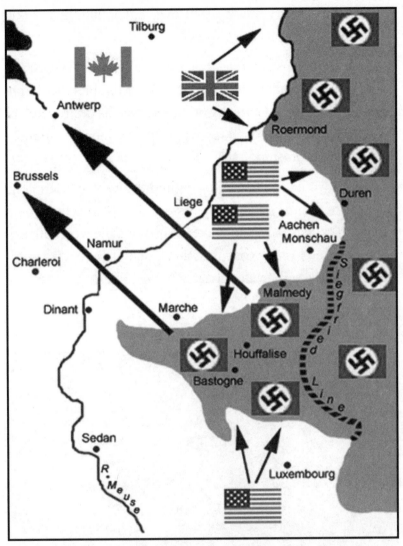

The German counter attack in the Ardennes, December 1944

The view from Ron's Sexton during the Ardennes Campaign,
December 1944

Finally...

...the popular song's lyrics come true

The regiment in action

Chapter Eleven

Closing in

15th January - 8th May 1945

Since men first took up arms against each other, geography and terrain have influenced the strategies and tactics of military commanders, with seemingly insignificant landscapes becoming sites where the destiny of countless nations has been decided. Hills, rivers, valleys, forests, and other physical features have been utilised for attack and defence for thousands of years, and often, when employed effectively, they have either significantly influenced the course of the battle, or proved to be the deciding factor in the conflict. The battlefields of the Second World War were no different.

Since 6th June 1944, when the ramps of the landing craft first hit the sand of the Normandy beaches, the Allied troops had but one overriding goal, and that was to go forward. The millions of conferences, plans, orders, and messages, held and distributed throughout the campaign, were all designed with this principle in mind. For the troops on the ground this was a difficult, and very often deadly, operational blueprint. In the nine months since the launch of the campaign the onus to press forward had lain entirely with the Allies, and for every objective taken a heavy price had been paid. Despite possessing an overwhelming superiority in materiel strength, the Allied soldiers were obliged to attack positions that the German defenders had had years in which to prepare.

From the hedgerows of Normandy to the flooded fields of Holland, the Allied advance had been a combination of a battle not only with the German Army, but also with the elements. It was a situation that had exhausted the men, but now, in February 1945, after all the months of hard slog and misery, the Rhine itself was finally within striking distance. The last barrier between the Allies and the German heartland was almost within reach. It was time for Operation Veritable to begin.

A glance at the map prior to Veritable's launch showed the Allied line strung out along the German border from France in the south, through Luxembourg and Belgium, to Holland in the north. Admittedly, some parts of German soil had already been captured, (most notably around Aachen, in the south), but on the whole the Allies were now ranged immediately in front of the Westwall, which was to be the focus of the German's last stand west of the Rhine.

The Allied commanders knew full well that finding a crossing over the Rhine intact would be extremely unlikely, and that they would need a secure area of operations before the mammoth task of constructing their own bridges over the river could begin. Vast quantities of engineers and equipment would need to be transported to the sites, and it would not be prudent to have enemy troops still operational in the rear areas. For this reason, it was imperative that all the remaining German forces between the Meuse and the Rhine be destroyed. Herein lay the essence of Operation Veritable.

On 15th January, three weeks before Veritable began, 86th Field Regiment had returned to the camp at Diest, near Brussels, for a rest and maintenance period, following their exertions in the Ardennes. The comfortable billets and the warm welcome from the locals were a pleasant contrast, and for the next two weeks the men occupied themselves with maintenance and painting, along with other obligatory regimental duties. A spell out of the firing line was always welcome, but it was the 'leave roster' that the men were anxious about. Considering the circumstances in which his leave had recently been cancelled, Ron fully expected to be the first on the list when it was reintroduced. He soon found out however, that this was not to be.

On 1st February the regiment said farewell to Diest, and with the rest of XXX Corps, began the journey north to Nijmegen, where troops and artillery were being assembled in secrecy for the coming offensive. A polluted water supply at a rest stop on route saw many of the gunners contract dysentery, which made the remainder of the journey even more tortuous than usual.

For the better part of the next week the men began stealthy preparations for Veritable, from the regimental harbour area on the fringe of the Groesbeek Forest. All around them in the Nijmegen bridgehead, dozens of similar units were doing the same.

> *"I don't remember much about heading up to Nijmegen, but it would have been like all the other big operations; you knew when something really big was happening. There'd be tanks, trucks, guns, troops, and every piece of equipment you could think of. Traffic jams and lack of space were always a problem wherever we went."*

By the evening of 7th February XXX Corps, which was to play the major part in the assault, was ready to go. Augmented by a variety of other units, the corps now consisted of approximately

202

200,000 men. In the darkness of the bridgehead, six infantry divisions, one armoured division (the Guards), three armoured brigades, eleven units from the 79th Armoured Division (Hobart's Funnies), and a vast array of artillery were ready. Ahead of them, the troops of the German First Parachute Army lay huddled in their trenches, pillboxes, and fortified villages. The pulverising bombing by the Allied planes was miserable enough to endure, but at this point they knew nothing of the man-made hurricane that was about to descend upon them.

Operation Veritable was one arm of a giant pincer movement. The other, Operation Grenade was an American venture, and if all went as planned, these pincers would snap together near the Rhine, sealing the fate of any surviving Germans caught inside. With First Canadian Army (to which XXX Corps was attached), pressing from the north, and Ninth United States Army advancing from the south, the Germans would be trapped in the pocket, with their backs to the river. If the Allies could move fast enough, it was even hoped that the important bridge at the town of Wesel might be captured intact.

This was the plan; no one doubted that it would be tough going. The route that XXX Corps would take to the Rhine meant attacking through the heavily defended Reichswald Forest (a key section of the Siegfried Line), and capturing the fortified towns of Cleve and Goch, on the other side of it. All three of these objectives were formidable defensive points, but it was the forest itself that held most fears for the attackers. Nine miles long by five miles wide, and criss-crossed with roads totally unsuitable for heavy armour; this dense, dark woodland had one good road that skirted around its northern perimeter. Understandably, this was the route chosen for the main assault.

"That forest was a bloody horrible place. The trees were so thick that no sunlight at all got through. Everything was dark and wet. We hated it."

To compound the lack of a good road network, temperatures had risen slightly towards the end of January, resulting in a thaw. As the corps formed up on the night of 7th January, some roads were already under water and many were collapsing under the weight of the men and machines. All this, and the battle hadn't yet started. Somewhere in the midst of this about-to-be-unleashed juggernaut, were the men of 86th Field Regiment. Their role in the 'show' would be to support 6 Guards Armoured Brigade, under command of 15th (Scottish) Infantry Division, as it attacked towards Kranenburg, a village just a few miles short of Cleve.

At 04.30 the following morning, 8th February, the still-dark sky was split asunder by one of the most ferocious artillery bombardment yet fired by the British Army in the war. 1,300 guns began pouring high explosive into the German positions. The 'Milk Round' had started.

"You never get used to a sound like that. It was deafening. We were throwing everything at them, but they still managed to shell us a bit too.

There was an Irish lad in our troop, Stanton his name was. He'd had this 'Dear John' letter from his missus, you know, she was leaving him. Well, our C.O.,

Fanshawe, gave him compassionate leave so that he could get home for a few days. The thing was, he came from Southern Ireland, so he had to wear 'civvy' clothes home, 'cos if he went back in uniform he might be targeted.

There was always a bit of shelling going on, so this night, before he left, we'd dug a trench as usual, big enough for six of us to sleep in. We had to wake each other every two hours for guard duty, and that's how someone found out that he'd been hit. They went to wake him, but it was too late. He was dead. He had a big shell splinter sticking out of his head."

At 10.30, with the barrage still in progress, the infantry attacked. The terrible ferocity of the Allied bombardment had stunned the Germans, making them no match for the Allied troops, who by the end of the first day, had taken over 1,000 prisoners. In the area in which the 86th was operating, the infantry had fought through terrible conditions (and without much of its tank support due to the boggy ground) but had succeeded in capturing the villages of Frasselt and Kranenburg, only 3 miles from Cleve.

The deteriorating conditions and natural grimness of the terrain combined to make life hell for the men. By the 9th the flooding was seriously jeopardizing the operation as a whole. The thaw, steady rain, and sheer volume of XXX Corps traffic, were turning every road, path, and track into a morass. The exhausted infantry had at times to wade through several feet of water, while many of the vehicles could not move at all.

Despite the mud, rain, and traffic, the Allies pressed on. On the morning of the 10th they reached the outskirts of Cleve where all Hell was let loose as the defenders sprang into action. All day long the battle raged, and by the next morning the historic town, reputed to be the birthplace of the legendary hero Siegfried, was nothing but a shattered ruin. Amongst the rubble and the shell holes, lay scores of casualties from both sides.

"Cleve is one of the places that I remember from that time. We had quite a battle there. By the time we went into the town later, everything was knocked to hell. It was the same old story, but there was no other way."

While Cleve was being contested, the battle in the forest itself wore on. In impossible conditions, the infantry and armour of both sides had met head-on in the claustrophobic, dripping woods, and a terrible fight was now in progress. Hundreds of Allied tanks had been assembled to breach the Siegfried Line here, but the Westwall lived up to its reputation and held out. It wasn't until the 10th, in the Frasselt area that the tanks of 44th Brigade Group succeeded in piercing the line, allowing the infantry to overrun the positions and gain a foothold in the area.

Now the Allies were in business. The Westwall had been breached, and the Reichswald Forest and Cleve had been occupied. The objective now was to push 8 miles southeast towards Calcar, which itself was only twenty miles from Wesel. 341 Battery of the 86th was assigned to take part in this action but German opposition was so strong along the route that the advance was called off, and the 15th Division was ordered to move on Goch instead, along with the rest of XXX Corps.

The town of Goch, 3 miles south of the southern edge of the Reichswald Forest, and practically along the centre line of the Allied advance, was a key road and rail junction, and therefore well defended. For the attack, artillery would once again play a key role, and on the 16th the guns of the 86th joined numerous similar units, and moved up to a point roughly halfway between Cleve and Goch. Two days later, on the morning of the 18th February, the 15th Division began the attack on Goch, finally winning control of the town three days later on the 21st.

> *"Goch was very much like Cleve. We had to practically destroy the place to capture it. The Germans holding on to these places were fanatics. We had no choice."*

Over the next ten days XXX Corps continued to fight its way southwards and eastwards. On the 23rd February, the Americans had finally been able to launch Operation Grenade, and as they advanced northeast towards General Horrocks' force, the previously mentioned pincers began to close around the remaining German troops still west of the river.

It had been costly. The desperate fighting had seen the Allies suffer over 6,000 casualties; 4,500 of them British; but their foe had also suffered at least as many. Further, and most significantly, 11,000 Germans were now marching westwards into captivity. The race to reach Wesel was now intensifying and for the next few days the regiment continued to support attacks being made southwards, in particular towards Kervenheim, during which, a mortar bomb that landed on his tank killed Captain Wood, A Troop commander.

"We didn't really see a lot of the other batteries, but it was always sad to hear that one of the troops had lost someone. The thing is, even though 341 and 462 Batteries were usually in the same general area as us, they were never in the same gun positions as us, so we didn't have a lot of contact. When, on the odd occasion we did meet, we got on fine. There was always a bit of good-natured competition between the batteries.

It was when someone in your own troop was killed that got to you the most. You missed them, of course you did. I'd come right through with boys like Stanton and John Leiper. We'd lived together day and night; we were like family, the whole troop. You just had to carry on the best you could."

On 2nd March new orders arrived. The guns were to move southwards as part of a thrust by the Guards Armoured Division along the XXX Corps left flank. Near the village of Geldern, approximately 15 miles east of the Wesel crossings, the force would join with the left flank of the American advance, and together they would head east toward the river. In their way were the fortified villages of Kapellen and Bonninghardt, and the resistance offered by the German parachute units defending them was bitter. It was not until the early hours of the 7th March that the last Germans were cleared from Bonninghardt.

Now, with the Allies only eight miles from Wesel, the Germans were once again trapped in a 'pocket', a reminder of the summer before, when thousands of their comrades had become ensnared

208

during the Allied breakout from the beachhead. This time though, the retreat was more orderly and as they fell back towards the bridges they exacted a heavy toll on the men and machines pursuing them. German 88mms continued to prove how effective they were against Allied armour, and for every mile gained there was the familiar sight of burning tanks and other vehicles; along with the dead of both sides.

As the Allied ring began to close, the guns of the 86th were kept busy supporting the advance of the 6 Guards Armoured Brigade into the centre of the 'pocket'. On the evening of 9th March the Coldstream Guards, supported by the regiment's guns, captured Menzelen, the last village in their path before Wesel. The remaining Germans were now streaming over the bridges to the east bank of the Rhine, where for a time they could gain a brief respite.

The Allies did all they could to stop them but the following morning on 10th March the Germans detonated the explosives attached to the Wesel bridges, sending them crashing down into the great river. This action signalled the end of Operation Veritable, and unlike Market-Garden it had been a success. With the two opposing armies now facing each other on either side of the Rhine the stage was set for the final battle.

The last six weeks of the war in northwest Europe followed a familiar pattern. The outcome of the conflict had never been in any serious doubt since the German retreat in the Ardennes. Hitler's reckless squandering of Germany's last reserves of men and materiel in that battle had left his armies severely under strength and lacking in every conceivable item of equipment, especially and most importantly, ammunition and fuel for the panzer formations.

Since then, the joint operations, Veritable and Grenade, had badly mauled his remaining forces and driven them back over the Rhine. As a result, the Allied line now ran from Nijmegen in the north, to the recently captured city of Cologne, 100 miles away to the south. If this wasn't bad enough for the Nazi leader, another event occurred that had sent him into a pathological rage. In prelude to the battle, he had issued an express command that all bridges over the Rhine were to be demolished if they came under imminent threat from the Allied advance. Incredibly, the order had not been carried out properly.

On 7th March US forces had made the startling discovery that the Ludendorff Bridge that spanned the Rhine at Remagen was still intact. Within hours that same day American units had reached and overwhelmed the German garrison there. Then, after beating off a German attempt to destroy the bridge they had raced over to the east bank and secured a small bridgehead. A major crossing had been gifted to the Americans and they were not slow to exploit it. Within ten days, amid furious German attempts to destroy it by artillery, three infantry divisions and one armoured had crossed the river and expanded the bridgehead considerably.

This tremendous achievement had given the Allies a foothold on the eastern bank, but it did not diminish the need for a crossing in the north of the line by the British and Canadians under Montgomery. That front had always been considered to be the most favourable route into the heartland of Germany, and now even more so, as the German forces in the area, the First Parachute Army, had been severely depleted after the recent battles. 'Monty' planned to hit them hard again as soon as possible, and as Veritable was coming to an end he unveiled the plan for the crossing of the Rhine on Twenty-First Army Group's front.

The first part of the plan was to launch amphibious units across the river at two sites opposite the towns of Rees and Wesel. Once these forces had reached the eastern bank, they were to secure the area and establish a bridgehead for the next stage of operations. With a point on each bank secure, the engineers could then begin the construction of large pontoon bridges, which would enable the follow up forces to cross. Four divisions of XII Corps would attack towards Wesel, while XXX Corps, with its five divisions, would make the assault towards Rees.

Prior to the attack Allied planes would fly 16,000 sorties, dropping 50,000 tons of bombs on the German positions, which would then be targeted by a 3,000-gun artillery barrage. The morning after the initial river-borne assault, two airborne divisions would be dropped about five miles inland from the east bank of the river, and secure roads and bridges to help strengthen the fledgling bridgehead. The planning of Operation Plunder was complete, now it was time to put it into action.

On 11th March, while Montgomery was putting the finishing touches to 'Plunder', the men and guns of 86th Field Regiment were ordered to move out of the line for a few days, but to remain in the area of Bonninghardt, about seven miles west of Wesel. The men used the time for maintenance and rest as once again the exertions of prolonged battle and living rough had taken its toll on them. Operation Veritable had been as demanding a battle as they had fought and it was testament to the men's resilience that their performance level had remained high throughout the operation. After three days at the camp, a new move was ordered; this time into billets at Nijmegen where the men carried out extensive maintenance duties over the course of the next six days.

Away to the southeast, on the twelve-mile front between Rees and Wesel, an enormous man-made fog had descended. This smoke screen was vital to the build up for Operation Plunder as it was very important that the Germans didn't discover where the assault would take place. The whole area on the west bank was teeming with men and equipment, but the Germans on the far bank couldn't see them. Knowing that the Allies would attempt a crossing at some point, the German artillery fired shells hopefully across the river, but to counter this, Allied aircraft roamed the skies looking for any targets that might interfere with the preparation for 'Plunder'.

At night endless columns of trucks brought men and materials up to the assault area, where in the moonlight the camouflage units worked like Trojans to conceal the build up. 30,000 tons of equipment, and hundreds of engineers were brought in to assemble the bridges necessary to carry the Allied advance forward. First though, the troops had to get across and gain a foothold. On XXX Corps front the units chosen to carry out the opening assault were elements of the 51st (Highland) Division, which had recently been practising waterborne assaults on the Maas River in preparation for 'Plunder'. It was an apt code-name, as 'souvenir-hunting' amongst every army involved in the conflict was a favourite past time. Some of the men though, took it to the extreme.

"Some of the boys were terrible. We had one bloke who was a real terror. He'd take anything, even off dead soldiers. If he saw a watch or a ring on a dead German, he wouldn't think twice about cutting the whole finger off if need be. I mean, I had my share of stuff, but I never did anything like that.

We had some bad buggers in the British Army. People talk about the Germans, but from my experiences the average Wehrmacht soldier was all right; it was the SS that were the bastards."

Back at Nijmegen, the 86th received orders to travel south to a marshalling area on the southern tip of the Reichswald Forest. For the operation the regiment had been placed under command of 51st Division, so plans were drawn up as to the order in which the Sextons and the other vehicles would make the crossing. The start date of 'Plunder' was drawing near and on the night of 21st March all of the artillery units that were to take part in the initial barrage were called forward to their gun positions. For the 86th this meant travelling ten miles to a small village three miles south of Rees.

Due to the volume of military traffic and the strict light

discipline, the journey took much longer than it normally would, so it wasn't until 04.00 on the morning of the 22nd that the men finally arrived at their destination. Tired as they were by this point, there was still work to be done and it was only after camouflaging the vehicles that the men were allowed to rest.

After catching up on some sleep, the remainder of 22nd March and the following day were taken up with preparations for the imminent river assault. During 'Veritable' huge ammunition and fuel dumps had been created along the route of the advance, and now the artillery units that were to take part in the opening bombardment busied themselves ferrying shells to the gun positions, digging trenches, and stocking up on any other piece of equipment and rations they would need.

During the afternoon of the 23rd, the attack began. Three thousand guns erupted in a deafening roar, and for the next few hours the Germans once again suffered from the awesome might of the Allied artillery and air superiority. At nine o'clock, as the Germans lay huddled in their trenches. the river assault began. In the darkness the barges, 'Buffaloes' (amphibious tracked vehicles), and sixty-ton tank-carrying ferries began heading for the far bank with their cargoes of troops and equipment. Everywhere, the night was punctuated with the sound of battle, and lit by the deceptive beauty of tracer fire, now zipping in both directions.

German resistance was weak. The artillery and bombers had done their job well. Some barges and 'dukws' were sunk or holed, but the main force soon reached the far side of the river and established a perimeter around the proposed bridgehead site. As soon as confirmation of the success was received the engineers of the British Army set to work, and due to their tremendous skill and resilience (they worked under shell-fire the whole time), seven bridges were operational by the afternoon of the 26th. Thanks to this incredible achievement, eight British and Canadian divisions had crossed the river by the following day, and after linking up with the airborne troops that had landed that morning they began to expand the bridgehead.

The speed with which the bridges had been built led to a change of plan for the 86th. The original plan to split the batteries up and send them over the river by ferry was now discarded. Instead, it was decided that the regiment would cross together, by means of the recently completed 'London Bridge' at Rees. As the S.P.s and trucks rumbled over the river a sense of exhilaration and accomplishment swept over the men.

"We'd had to hang around for a while, waiting for the engineers to finish the bridge. We were just taking pot shots at anything that moved on the other side of the river. It was quite a nice day if I remember. I've got a photograph of me and a couple of lads, lying on the riverbank, with the new bridge in the background. Once we got the word that we could cross it was great. We really felt that we were on our way. You couldn't help but think, 'It can't be long now'.

Once we got over to the other side we went straight into Rees. It was in a bad state. I remember seeing the

215

warning sign there, 'YOU ARE NOW ENTERING GERMANY, AN ENEMY COUNTRY. BE ON YOUR GUARD."

Once across the Rhine the regiment took part in operations to expand and secure the bridgehead firing from the village of Millengen. The following day they moved again, and were reunited with the Guards Armoured Division, which was about to begin the drive northeast towards the port of Bremen, over one hundred miles away.

While the British and the Canadians headed north and northeast, the Americans to their south, began the encirclement of the enemy forces in the Ruhr. By 1st April 350,000 German troops were surrounded in this industrial wasteland by two US armies. Further north, the usual problem of traffic made for a slow start for the Guards Armoured Division, but within a few hours they reached open ground and the advance gained momentum.

By the morning of 31st March the division had reached Dinxperlo, just inside the southern tip of the Dutch border.

German resistance was constant but uneven. Roadblocks, blown bridges, and small actions against groups armed with panzerfausts caused delays, but rarely for long. The advance soon took a familiar pattern; villages and towns would be entered, secured, and then left behind, while the Guards moved on to tackle the next objective.

On 2nd April the division turned east again and made for the German border. That night, leading elements arrived in the town of Nordhorn, and it was here that a new problem emerged.

Reports were coming in that twenty miles to the east, where the river Ems flowed through the town of Lingen, the retreating Germans had sabotaged the canal bridge, despite desperate efforts by the Guards reconnaissance units.

This was a problem. Lingen was heavily defended and the only other crossing was at the village of Ems, three miles downstream. Defended by German troops with machine-guns, three 88mm anti-tank guns, and prepared for demolition if the need arose, the Lingen bridge was a formidable obstacle. Despite this, the Guards set out to capture it.

In the early hours of 3rd April the attack force was in place, overlooking the bridge. Further back, at the allotted time, the guns of 86th Field Regiment opened up. Under the cover provided by the artillery and their own tanks, the men of the Coldstream Guards stormed the crossing. Once the western defences were overcome, Captain Liddell climbed under the bridge and cut the wires to the demolition charges. The award of the Victoria Cross later recognized his extraordinary bravery.

The advance was under way again. Later that day, Lingen itself was also secured, but due to the fanaticism of some of the German defenders, it wasn't until the 6th that the shattered town was totally cleared. It was during this battle that 342 Battery lost another one of its members, and it was in particularly tragic circumstances.

"The British Army had this system during the war where you could 'claim' your brother. What that meant was, if you were serving in the army and you had a

younger brother who was also a soldier, you could get him transferred to your unit. This happened with a lad in our battery, Fred Ager, his name was. He had a younger brother, Ron, and Fred claimed him so he could keep an eye on him and look after him.

Well, this day we were firing as usual; we were right on the edge of a wood, and further back behind us there was a battery of Bofors guns, which were anti-aircraft guns. As we were firing there was a 'tree burst', and Ron Ager got hit. What had happened was one of the 40mm shells from a Bofors had fallen short, and showered the battery area with shrapnel. Ron was killed outright. I can't imagine how his brother felt."

Bremen was getting closer. Occasionally, a town or village was approached and found deserted, such as Lengerich, which was reached on 7th April, but on the whole there was usually some kind of resistance along the whole route. Even the most ardent Nazis must have realised the inevitability of an Allied victory by now, but this did not deter many German soldiers from continuing to do their duty under the most severe strain. Because of this casualties continued to mount on both sides, with the 86th incurring their share. Three more of the regiment's members, Gunners Mckay and Gibb, and Corporal Hucknall, had been killed on 8th April, all three victims of 88mm shellfire.

In the east and the west, the Allied advance rolled on. On the Guards Armoured Division front, Herbergen, Menslage (where the regiment blew the church steeple to pieces), and Boen all fell by 11th April. By the 14th the division had reached Cloppenburg, less than forty miles away from Bremen. They were due shortly to move to another corps and went into a rest area, with 86th Field Regiment, who moved into billets in nearby Westerenstek. It was a temporary rest for the gunners because three days later they were thrown back into the fray, this time with 51st Division, which was preparing to attack the town of Delmenhorst, eight miles from Bremen.

On the 20th, in preparation for the assault on Delmenhorst, the Sextons moved to new positions. A long journey ensued, which turned out to be in vain due to a successful British operation conducted the day before. The next objective however, would definitely have to be fought for. Bremen, the sister port of Hamburg lay astride the River Weser, which flowed north into the larger River Elbe, the agreed meeting point between the Russians attacking from the east, and the Allies approaching from the west.

It was a city steeped in history, and had been an important cultural centre before the war, but now it was no more than a hollow shell. Being one of the largest ports in Germany, and housing U-Boat pens and aircraft factories, it had received particular attention from the Allied bombers. Nevertheless, amid the ruined buildings, and rubble-strewn streets the defenders rejected an Allied offer for them to surrender the town without bloodshed.

The war might be coming to an end but many German troops, especially the Waffen SS, fought on. Their devotion to duty may have been admirable, but as usual it was the civilian population that suffered. Every major city in Germany had by this point been practically destroyed, leaving the inhabitants without sanitation, water, food, and shelter. The result was an exodus.

"The amount of refugees we were seeing was unbelievable. There were loads and loads; it was a pitiful sight really. Men, women, and children of all ages, the roads were full of them. They were running away from the Russians, and some of them had packed prams and carts with anything that they'd managed to save in time.

Our tank columns stretched for hundreds and hundreds of yards and I'm sure that some hit these refugees. There was just so many of them."

Once they realised that they would have to fight their way into the town the Allies unleashed no less than four divisions, which attacked from every direction. At the same time massed artillery, including the guns of the 86th, began pouring shells into the stricken city. Although under intense pressure the Germans managed to hold out for three days, but the outcome was never in any doubt, and by 26th April Bremen was in Allied hands. It had been a bloody battle, and once again the 86th suffered casualties. Bombardier Waterton of 341 Battery was killed by shellfire on the 25th, and two other members, Lieut. Coultas, and Gunner Wilson, who had been missing for days, were found dead as a result of their jeep setting off a mine.

The closer the end of the war seemed the more nervous Ron got.

He had long since learned not to take stupid risks but danger was still ever present.

"You'd say to yourself, 'Am I going to get through? Are they going to get me before the end?' You try to be a bit more careful, but you can't really. My attitude was, 'You've got to do it'. Your mates keep you going, and to be honest, you're cocky at that age. I got through unscathed, which is amazing really considering the amount of action that we saw."

After Bremen had been secured the next objective for XXX Corps was Cuxhaven, an important naval base to the north. Over the next few days the armoured column continued to head north, and was occasionally troubled by sporadic, disorganised opposition, but as April gave way to May even this token resistance crumbled. German troops were giving themselves up everywhere, and the 86th had little firing to do in their support of 51st Division's advance to Bremerhaven and Cuxhaven. By now, rumours of a German surrender were sweeping through the rank and file of every unit, along with the astonishing news that Adolf Hitler himself was dead.

"The rumours were the usual stuff. 'We'll be home for Christmas', that kind of thing. It never happened though! The best information we ever got was from the radio on the tank. Even though we weren't supposed to, sometimes if we had a quiet five minutes we'd turn to the BBC World Service broadcast, which was right up to date. That was the only way we ever found anything out.

I can't remember exactly when it was but it was around that time that we came across a concentration camp. Of course we didn't know what it was at the time, we just got a call from an infantry unit we were supporting asking our regiment for assistance.

I remember we travelled up a long road, with trees down the sides, and then there were big gates with machine-gun towers on either side.

We thought that it was just a POW camp, another stalag, but we soon found out that it was something completely different. We could smell this terrible stench, but we thought it was dead cattle 'cos we'd been used to that in Normandy.

What I saw in there turned my guts. I could stick pretty much anything, I still can now, but that place was terrible. I felt such anger. I never felt anger like that before, not even on D-Day; it's not like being in combat.

We weren't there long, thank God. We just stayed long enough for the infantry to secure the place and get everything sorted out with the higher authorities. We left then, and I'll tell you, I was glad to come from there."

With their fuhrer gone, their cities in ruins, and over two million of their soldiers lying dead on the battlefields of Europe, the German people now faced total defeat. The British and Canadian advance north had destroyed or cut off the remaining German forces in Holland, the US First and Ninth Armies had taken 325,000 prisoners in the Ruhr pocket, and on 2nd May the Red

Army had captured the capital, Berlin, after weeks of savage fighting. It was almost over.

As far as the 86th was concerned, the bullets stopped flying on 5th May. On other fronts the fighting would continue for days (months in the case of the Pacific), but for Twenty-First Army Group the war was over. At their billets in the village of Lintig, near Cuxhaven, the men of the 86th finally got the news that they had been waiting to hear for months. It was a sweet feeling.

"Well if I remember rightly, we were at the gun position. We knew that there were talks going on, but we were still seeing a bit of action. At some point it came over the tannoy that all German forces in our area had surrendered, and that it would take effect the following morning.

A big cheer went up and everybody was really excited, but to be honest, we couldn't celebrate too much 'cos they kept us on 'stand to' for about ten days after. We still had to be very vigilant because there were so many Germans still out there with all sorts of weapons.

We did have a party later on, and we made up for it then! It was such a relief to know that you'd got through alright."

All that the men wanted now was to get home. They had done their bit; indeed, served with distinction, but for those who were expecting to be leaving in the next few weeks, there was a shock in store. Germany was in a mess and nobody was going anywhere until it was sorted out. Ron included.

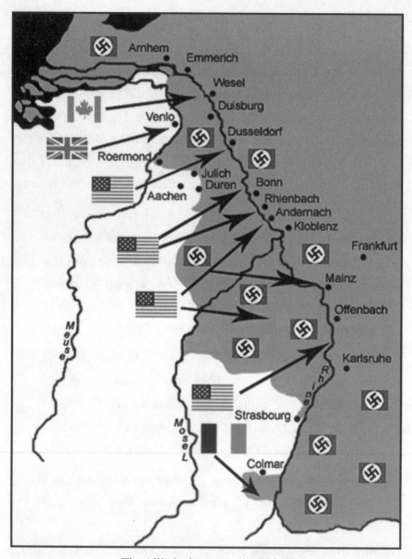

The Allied advance to the Rhine

Billet in a farmyard - Bremen

Some of 342 Battery posing with a Sherman of 86th Field Regiment

Fred Ager - who lost his brother
Ron in Germany

The Herts Stag Canteen
after a busy night!

342 Battery crossing 'London Bridge' at Rees, Germany 1945

Mons, Benny, Ron, Ginger & Jock
coming out of the line - Germany 1945

Germany during the summer of 1945
Ron is standing, far right

Chapter Twelve

Keeping a promise

8th May 1945 - Present day

It had been less than a year since the Allies had landed on the beaches of Normandy. At that time, two mighty armies had faced each other, consisting mainly of men who only a few years earlier had been civilians. Since then, many of them had seen and done things that they would never be able to come to terms with. War had changed them - forever.

By the time the German surrender was ratified on 8th May 1945, the 86th Field Regiment had had three days to get used to the idea that the war was over. Amid the joyous atmosphere the officers had to remind the gunners that they still had a job to do, which began with a move to Cuxhaven to help in the disarmament of the German forces there, and the dismantling of a V1 experimental facility.

On 18th May the regiment moved to the area of Verden, which unknown to them would be their home for the next year or so. The three villages of Stedorf, Dorverden, and Westen, were used to accommodate the men, and due to the recent fighting, much of the men's time was taken up with repairing and cleaning the shattered buildings.

The summer months were a mixture of work and play. Processing refugees, and inspections and searches of the surrounding area, were some of the tasks undertaken by the men, but they also had a lot of free time. Wisely, the army provided plenty of distractions for them in the shape of sports, films and other entertainment. Further, the men took it upon themselves to refurbish the local pub, which was renamed 'The Hertfordshire Stag', and it soon became a very popular meeting point for the whole regiment!

"Around that time the Luneburg trials were going on. It was the town where Hitler had his very first big rally before the war. They were trying the Nazi war criminals there, and a few people from the regiment were allowed to go and watch it in the public gallery. Well, as luck would have it, I found out our Fred was in charge of the guard there, so I went to this officer, Smallman his name was, and I told him.

He wasn't a bad bloke, I used to give him Capstan Full Strength cigarettes; he loved them! Anyway, he told me that I had to put my name up, and if I was pulled out of the hat I'd be able to go. He said he had to be fair about it.' 'That's OK', I said, but I didn't think there was much chance of me going 'cos the whole regiment was involved, and only six people could go at any one time!

Anyway, the next night I was lying in bed and this bloke comes up to me and says, 'Come on, you're on detail'. I said, 'what are you on about? I've only just finished!' ' Well, it's definitely you', he said."

Ron was not amused by this interruption, but he wasn't about to start disobeying orders at this point in his army career, so off he went to the guardroom to find out what was going on.

"I got to the guardroom, and this bloke said to me, 'You're duty driver for the next trip to Luneburg Heath'. Great! I thought; Smallman had got me in. Now my only problem was getting into the court, 'cos as duty driver you didn't get a court pass. There was a

*big American MP on the gate when we arrived and
I knew I had no chance of getting past him!*

*The thing was, I could see our Fred through the gates,
but this MP didn't want to know. There was another one
there though, and he told me to go around the back. Off
I went, and when I got round the back I saw a couple
of soldiers waiting outside this building. 'Hey mate, are
you Duke of Cornwall Light Infantry?' I said, and they
said they were. 'Do you know Sergeant Hamilton?' I
said, and they said 'Yeah, he's just come in'."*

Ron quickly explained to the troops that Sergeant Hamilton was
his brother. They were more than happy to help him.

*"One of them shouted 'Sergeant, we've caught
someone moping about outside!' and our Fred said,
'Bring him in!' Well, he very nearly died!"*

After getting over the shock of seeing his baby brother, Fred
organized some sandwiches and cocoa ("They were cocoa
bloody mad in the army"), and over the impromptu snack the
brothers chatted about everything that had happened to them
over the last few months. Afterwards Fred took Ron into the
balcony to watch the trial.

*"They were trying Herma Grees while I was there.
She'd been in charge of the camp at Buchenwald.
Rumour had it that she used to walk around the camp
very near naked and if any of the inmates even looked
at her she'd set dogs with spiked collars on them.*

Apparently her lampshades were made out of human

232

skin. She wasn't a bad-looking girl either; it was hard
to believe that she could do something like that. There
was another bloke on trial as well, a fellow called
Krammer. He had a scar from one ear to the other; it
looked like someone had tried to cut his throat."

August 11th was a defining day, as it was the day that the
Sextons were handed back to ordnance. The men had worked
very hard sprucing up the vehicles, and when they had finished
they looked like they'd never been used. Looks can be deceiving.

Over the next few months, transfers to and from the regiment
were commonplace. Some men were sent to the Far East, while
new faces arrived from other regiments. The 'de-mob' process
was painfully slow, and Christmas 1945 came and went without
Ron receiving any news as to when he would be going home.

Finally, in the second week of March 1946, news came.

"I finally got out on a 'B' Class, on 12th March 1946.
That stood for Building Worker, and because of my job
before, I was sent home to help repair the damage
caused by the war. Fair play, they even changed the
date so that I could get home for my birthday, which
was the 13th!

I got my kit together, said goodbye to my mates and
travelled by train to Ostend, where I caught a boat to
Harwich. From there, I had to go to the 'de-mob'
centre in Aldershot, which was the main depot. The
only things you were allowed to keep were your
discharge papers and your will; everything else, your

uniform, equipment, even your 'dog-tags', had to be
handed in.

I was given a 'civvy suit', and some money and off I
went. No one at home knew I was coming home. I
caught a train to Lime Street Station, but the ferry to
Wallasey had gone, so I caught the one to Birkenhead
instead. From there I went to the local police station to
find out if there were any buses at that time of night."

There weren't, but whether the policeman felt sorry for Ron, or
he was just glad to help a soldier coming home, he gave him a
cup of cocoa and told him to go and sit down.

"Well this policeman offered to drive me as far the four
bridges. He must have phoned the station in Wallasey,
'cos when we got to the bridge, the Wallasey police
were waiting to take me the rest of the way home! I
was very grateful for that. Well, they took me to the
corner of Trafalgar Road, and even though it was
nighttime, I walked down Lee Road singing and
whistling! I was so chuffed to be home!

When I got to my mam's, I banged on the door, and cos
it was late all the neighbors were popping their heads
out of their windows to see what was going on. Well,
down comes my dad with his 'long johns' on, and when
he opened the door he nearly had a heart attack! Then
my mam hears my voice, and she comes down the
stairs like a bloody whippet!
I'd kept my promise."

234

Once his mother and father had got over the shock of seeing Ron home again, he had another surprise for them.

"In the fuss I'd forgotten that I had all this stuff in my bag. I'd brought a pure silk tablecloth home for my mother. I'd taken it from a derelict shop in Germany; 'That's for my mam', I thought!

After I'd given her that, I showed my dad what else I had. My kit bag was half-full of cigarettes! My dad was pleased cos at that time the most you could get at home was five at a time. The next day my dad had to go to work, but I went up the Nelson! He met me there later on and we had a great time.

A few weeks later, our Fred came home, too. He didn't know that I'd been de-mobbed, and he had a hell of a shock! It was great to see each other."

Now, as the initial euphoria of being home subsided, the task of re-adjusting to civilian life began. After a few weeks things settled down and Ron returned to working as a builder on the numerous bomb-damaged buildings in the Liverpool area. Around Christmas time that year, Ron's uncle passed away, and it was at the funeral that he met his future wife, Joan. They began courting, and within a year they were married. Not long after, Ron decided to become a member of the British Legion.

"Well, by this point Joan was having our Ronnie, and I'd seen somewhere that if you became a member, you

got a free set of baby clothes and a cover for the pram. Joan said we should give it a go, so off I went up to Withins Lane and signed on the dotted line. I've been in it ever since."

For the next few years Ron continued to earn his living as a builder, and in 1948 the family moved to Ruyton XI Towns, Shropshire, where Ron had found a job at the nearby Park Hall building site. By this time Joan had had their second child, a girl they named Myra. In time Ron changed jobs and went to work at an army camp in Nescliffe. He worked in the RSD section for a while, where he was responsible for checking ammunition as it came in off the trains. Later, an opportunity arose for a transfer to the Fire Department at the site, where he was very happy for the next seven years.

"It was while I was at the fire service that someone started calling me Danny, after the entertainer, Danny Kaye. It just stuck, and now everyone calls me it. I don't think a lot of people even know that my real name is Ron. I loved that job. I was very sorry to leave it, but I had no choice cos they were closing the place down.

From there I went to work in a factory called Sankeys. We used to make all sorts of wheels there, and I'll tell you, it was like the black hole of Calcutta! 22 years I was there, and it was such a horrible place that when the chance for early retirement came along, I jumped at it."

However, retirement did not sit well with Ron and in time he took a job at the local hospital in Shrewsbury.

> *"Well, I took it to keep me occupied, and for a bit of pocket money. I was a car park attendant to start with, but after a bit I got a job as a porter in the maternity ward. That was the best job I ever had! I could have stopped there until I was 99! We used to have such a laugh."*

For people who know Ron, laughter is something that they associate him with. Despite the horrors he saw and endured as a young man, and setbacks he suffered in later life, he has always been kind and positive; something his children, Tina and Willy told me time and again.

> *"I was a founder member of the Normandy Veterans Association, and I've always been active in the British Legion, but I never talked about my time in the army for years and years. Mind you, I dreamt about it a lot, I still do. It was only on the 50th anniversary that I went back for the first time. A bloke I was working for was going over to Normandy, and he asked if I'd like to go, so I did.*
>
> *It has helped a lot talking about it. Doing this book has helped too, but there's still some stuff that you just want to leave behind."*

Danny and Joan still live in Shropshire, in a small village called Kinnerley. Their numerous grandchildren and great-grandchildren form a huge part of their life. In March of 2003,

'Danny' celebrated his eightieth birthday at a big party in the village hall. The number of people who attended is testament to his character, as is the fact that he was the last one standing at the end of the night!

He is a remarkable man.

Joan Penton

Joan with her and Ron's first
child, Ronnie

Ron, his mother, Ronnie and Myra

Ron looking dapper on New
Brighton Pier

Veterans of 86th Field Regiment at the ceremony to honour
them at Ver-sur-Mer, September 2002

L-R. Jolyon, Danny and Willy

The author at the Sexton memorial to 86th Field Regiment in Ver-sur-Mer

The author with Danny, September 2002

Joan and Danny as they are today

Bibliography

Hertfordshire Yeomanry Regiments, Royal Artillery, - (J D Sainsbury, 1999),

The Second World War in the West, - (Charles Messenger, 1999)

And we shall shock them, - (David Fraser, 1983)

Club Route, 30 Corps in Europe - (Ronald Gill and John Groves, 1946)

Overlord - (Max Hastings, 1984)

Ardennes, the secret war - (Charles Whiting, 1984)

Gold Beach, Inland from King - (Christopher Dunphie and Garry Johnson, 1999)

The Third Reich at War - (Michael Veranov, 1997)

The Penguin Atlas of D-Day - (John Man, 1994)

Brasso, Blanco, and Bull - (Tony Thorne, 1998)

Handbook of World War II - (Abbeydale Press, 1995)

The Beaches of D-Day - Editions, (Ouest, France, 2002)

Normandy Landing Beaches - (Major and Mrs Holts Battlefield Guide, 1999)

World War II - (Ivor Matanle, 1989)

The Macmillan dictionary of The Second World War - (Elizabeth-Anne Wheal and Stephen Pope, 1989)

The Battle of D-Day - (William Mcelwee, 1965)

Citizen Soldiers - (Stephen E Ambrose, 1997)

Band of Brothers - (Stephen E Ambrose, 1992)

D-Day and the Battle of Normandy - (Martin Windrow, 1995)

D-Day, June 6th, 1944 - (Stephen E Ambrose, 1995)

About the author

Simon Evans is a keen, amateur military historian. This is his second project; the first, 'Becoming Airborne' was written in 1999.

He lives in Laugharne, West Wales, with his wife Adele, son Harri, and daughter Hannah.